5 Steps to Achieving Happiness and a Positive Mindset

How to stop doubting your greatness, overcome your fears, take control of your life, be the best version of yourself, live a more successful life

Sharon J Moore

i

Sharon J Moore

Table of Contents

Sharon J Moore

Introduction

People have been striving daily to achieve a positive mindset amid all their troubles. Despite all the hardships we face and all the battles we lose, somewhere deep inside, we still believe that we are going to pull through and become better versions of ourselves in the future. Some world-famous people have overcome adversity in their lives, only to come out stronger and more resilient. Charlize Theron had witnessed her mother killing her abusive alcoholic father in self-defense when she was just 15 years old. Can you imagine experiencing something so sinister at such a young age? Charlize refused to let this trauma consume her life. She could have easily fallen prey to the negativity that came with this experience, but she rose above it and used all those feelings to catapult herself into a million-dollar career.

Oprah Winfrey is one of the most influential people in the

world, and she is the highest-paid African American woman of the 20th century, but her childhood and teenage years were far from happy. Oprah lived with her single mother in poverty, and they were physically abused often, including her uncle, cousin, and a family friend sexually abusing her. She had to wear dresses that were made from potato sacks. Oprah ran away from home at age 13 because she could no longer tolerate the abuse. She fell pregnant at age 14 and gave birth to a premature baby who died shortly after being born. This negative situation did not hold Oprah back. She studied hard and was successful in her academic ventures. Since she took public speaking at school, she did a few broadcasting jobs to help her start her career. Oprah faced many hurdles at the beginning of her career, but she never gave in to her failures and setbacks. She had a very clear picture of what she wanted to become in life, and she continued to work hard and chase her dreams. Her positive outlook and faith in a better future helped her become the successful woman she is today.

Sylvester Stallone, the handsome hunk from the *Rocky* and *Rambo* movie franchises, had his fair share of struggles before he rose to fame. At one stage in his life, Sylvester was so broke that he ended up homeless. He sold all of his wife's jewelry to survive, and he even had to sell his beloved dog for $25 because he could not afford to feed him any longer. He described that moment as the lowest he's ever been in his life.

Sylvester wrote the movie *Rocky* after he watched a boxing match where Mohamed Ali was fighting. This match inspired him to do something out of the ordinary, and so he took a chance on life. He sold his script to a well-known studio, and they agreed to let him star in the movie. The budget for the movie was only one million dollars, but it made $225 million at the box office. Sylvester is a good example of how life can get so hard before it becomes easy. He believed in himself, despite what everyone else said. Today, he is one of the most successful actors and directors around. The power of positive thinking can change your life in ways that you could have never imagined. I can understand that you have been through a lot in your life, but trials and tribulations come part and parcel with life, and there is no way that any of us could ever try to avoid it. As demotivating and discouraging as it can be, there is no way that you can just sit there and lose faith in yourself.

This book is going to show you five amazing steps you can follow to achieve a positive mindset that will help you overcome any situation. You can rise above your troubles and break through anything holding you back. It doesn't matter how old or young you are or what type of financial background you have; if you follow these five steps, they guarantee you a change in your mindset, and you can set yourself free from the bondage of depression and failure. This book will be your guide and support you on your journey to achieving a healthy mindset and a positive attitude. The only way you are ever going to achieve success is to stop making excuses and start taking action. Don't let fear and that negative voice in your head hold you back, switch it off and start listening to your heart. What do you truly desire? Do you believe in yourself? Or are you second-guessing yourself and questioning your capabilities? Whatever the situation is, whether you are confident in yourself or not yet, you can continue on this journey. Start motivating yourself. You don't need to wait for anyone to believe in you. As long as you have faith in yourself, you will make it happen.

CHAPTER 1

What Is Positive Thinking, and How Do I Achieve It?

Positive anything is better than negative nothing.
–Elbert Hubbard

The Power Of Positive Thinking

Being able to think positively in every situation is a remarkable skill that few of us possess. When life becomes too much to handle, it can seem impossible to think of a good outcome when you are standing amid difficulty. You may have heard people say that positive thinking will incite a positive outcome from the universe, especially when you need a solution to a problem that has been plaguing you for quite a while. You can never really know the power of positive thinking in your life unless you have experienced it firsthand, and going on the advice of others might seem like something out of a fable. Only when you see it happening in your own life, then you will attest to it. Let's explore the power of positive thinking further in this chapter.

What Does It Mean to Have a Positive Mindset and a Positive Attitude?

We all have come across one of those people in our lives who maintain a happy-go-lucky attitude no matter what may come their way. They always think positively and expect a good outcome out of every situation, even when it's hard to see any hope. It isn't because they are oblivious to the concerns that they are facing in their life; it is because they have the power to manifest positivity by reframing their thoughts. When you change the way you react to situations, you are also changing how you handle your problems, and the outcome will be different as well. Let's be realistic. No one is born with a positive attitude. It is something that is gained over the years as you go through life experiences. Being naturally optimistic and pessimistic when faced with difficulty isn't something that happens instinctively.

People who react positively to negative situations usually have to spend a lot of time working on creating a healthy mindset and a healthy attitude that will enable them to change the way they think and react to these situations. As they say, practice makes perfect, so as you face difficult situations in life, you can use these trials to help you become more positive and more hopeful. Change your outlook on the trials that you face, and you will see how much you can learn from them. We all should adopt a more open attitude, then we will be able to gain wisdom from our experiences. Life is too short to waste time on regrets and sorrow; instead, we should always try to make ourselves better people than we were yesterday.

Why Is It Important to Have a Positive Attitude?

In the same way that a coin has two sides, so does life. As human beings, we have a choice: either live out our lives with a positive outlook or just merely exist with a negative outlook. I use the phrase "merely exist" to emphasize that if you do not have a positive outlook and attitude, you may not be living life to the fullest. People don't just choose to be negative, rather, it is the circumstances of their lives that force them to take this approach. It is so important to have a positive attitude because your thoughts and your actions have the power to manifest greatness in your life. When you are facing one of the hardest trials you could ever experience, what good would it bring if you kept thinking negative thoughts? When you tell yourself things like, "I can't do this anymore" and "I have had it," are you really helping yourself in any way?

The answer is no! By using a negative thought pattern, you are only putting yourself down more and making the obstacle more difficult to overcome. Isn't it time you realized no matter how many times you try, if you don't embrace positivity, then there will not be any change? Negative behaviors will only warrant negative consequences. If you are always giving in to thoughts that limit you and your potential, there will be no positive outcome. Choosing to be positive is a moment-by-moment decision that you have to make since negativity always tries to worm its way back into your mind. A positive attitude helps you deal with stress and negativity daily. Being optimistic makes it easier to prevent stressing and overthinking about the concerns you have in life, which also prevents negative thinking.

Positivity is powerful enough to turn your life around for the better, just as negativity is powerful enough to destroy your life. I think it's pretty clear which is the wiser choice to make. You may wonder how a positive attitude and mindset manifest themselves in your life? If you haven't experienced it before, it could be difficult to make sense of it all; however, once you understand, I can guarantee that something within you will change, and you will want to follow the five steps in this book to become a better version of yourself.

Wise Parables About Positivity

Below are a few wise parables to help you gain a deeper

understanding of how positivity can work to your benefit and well-being. The stories in this book will inspire you and open up your mind to all the possibilities that are available to you as a positive person.

The Surprise Test

One day, a teacher entered the classroom and shocked all the students with an announcement. A surprise test was going to be given to them in a few minutes. All the students became anxious and confused because they were worried about what was going to be given in the test. They weren't prepared, and the fear of failure became clear among the students. The teacher walked around, passing out the test papers with the front side faced down. Once he had finished handing out the papers to all the students, he then asked them to turn over their test sheets and begin the test. As the students turned over their test sheets, confusion spread across the room. There were no questions printed on the sheet; nothing was on there except for a black dot in the center of the page.

The teacher then instructed the learners to write a few lines about what they saw on their sheet of paper. After being confused for a while, the students began writing because they had no choice. It was a test, after all. After everyone had finished, the teacher collected the answer sheets and began reading each one aloud to the class. All the learners had written about the black dot—they wrote about its position on the page, its size, its color, and how unnecessary it was. But none of the learners cared to write about the white, clean part of the paper. Our daily lives start with a plain white sheet of paper. We can observe the paper and learn as much as we can from it; however, we focus on the black dots instead.

There is so much to be grateful for—our family, our careers, our health, and our homes—but we still limit ourselves by focusing on the unpleasant experiences in life such as our failures, heartbreaks, missed opportunities, and frustrations. These things cloud our view and hinder us from seeing the bigger picture. These dark spots, as small as they are, still restrict us from thinking positively, and we lose sight of all the joyful experiences because of the trauma experienced by these negative situations. Every day may not be a good day, but there is something good in everyday life. Change the way you look at situations in your life; as the famous saying goes, "Don't see the glass as half-empty, instead, see it as half-full."

The Two Frogs

This is a story about two frogs who were stuck in a deep, dried-up well. Both frogs put in their best efforts to jump out of the well; however, none of them succeeded. The news of this spread and caught the attention of the other animals. They all gathered around the well to witness the two frogs struggling to get out. Most of the animals were shouting and telling them to stop trying because there was no way they would ever get out of the well and that they should just accept their fate and give up. After a few tries, one frog finally did just that by hitting his head against the wall until he was no longer breathing. But the other frog kept trying over and over to get himself out of the well. It was astonishing how headstrong he was. Jump after jump, he never gave up. After a gazillion tries, he had just enough strength left for one more jump.

This was it. He had reached the end, and now was the time for him to take that chance or simply just give up and die with the little strength he had left. The crowd of animals kept telling him how pointless it was for him to keep trying. They laughed at him and ridiculed his perseverance because they believed the frog had no chance of getting out of the well. The frog took his last jump. He put all of his strength and hope into this leap of faith, and he truly believed he could get himself out. His risk paid off, and he finally made it out of the well. The other animals were amazed at how the frog stayed strong and got himself out of the well, so they asked him how he did it. The frog did not reply to any of their questions. The reason being because the frog was deaf! Based on their facial expressions and gestures, he assumed they were cheering him on.

The frog thought that the other animals were encouraging him to stay strong and keep going, so he held on and gave it his all, and because of this, he survived and pushed forward despite the enormous obstacles in his way. So many people relate to the first frog in the story. When faced with adversity, they succumb to the opinions of others who don't even understand them. We often listen to what other people say about us, and this holds us back from taking the leap of faith that is required to succeed in life. All that is standing in the way of your success are the negative opinions of others. Be more like the second frog by turning a deaf ear to the negative remarks and use them as fuel to persevere and press on. Use the haters as your biggest motivators, and you will see the wonders of having a positive attitude.

How Does Positivity Affect Your Health?

Apart from using positivity to succeed in life, there are also umpteen ways that it can help improve your health significantly. We can see illness as something negative, and it can cause you to lose track of who you are, especially if you are experiencing a terminal illness that has caused you to lose hope for the future. The only way you can continue fighting for your life is if you use positivity to combat the negativity. Let's look at how maintaining a positive mindset can help you improve your health.

The Brain-Body Connection

The brain influences what goes on inside the body. I'm sure you must have experienced sweaty palms and pounding heartbeats whenever you were feeling anxious, and you must have developed a throbbing headache after constantly worrying and stressing over a situation. The brain and the body share a connection through neurotransmitters, chemicals, and hormones. The neurotransmitters are pathways that send signals from the brain to the body and vice versa to control our everyday functions such as our eating, walking, moving, thinking, and even our will, moods, and feelings as well. There are different parts of our brain responsible for different functions in our body. There is an emotional cortex that deals with feelings and emotions. The amygdala forms part of this cortex, and it regulates our feelings when faced with various situations. If you are facing a stressful situation, the brain can turn on your sympathetic nervous system, better known as the fight-or-flight response.

If you were being chased by a deadly animal, your brain would instantly turn on the fight, flight, or freeze response. This response helps us to deal with the situation that we are facing appropriately. In our response, we release hormones such as cortisol and adrenaline to help us fight the danger that we are facing. As these hormones release, our muscles tighten, we breathe faster, and our heart pounds faster. Our body responds similarly when we are very stressed and angry. Even though we are not facing any immediate threat, our brain has a hard time differentiating between physical distress and mental distress, causing it to release these hormones to enter the fight-or-flight response once again. Blood sugar and pressure rise as well, which causes the immune system to become suppressed. Additional symptoms of your body being in a fight-or-flight response are feeling dizzy, anxious, difficulty concentrating, shaking hands and trembling, feeling nauseated, and having the urge to go to the bathroom.

The Effects of Positive Emotions on Your Body

Just as your body responds to negative situations and emotions, your body also reacts when you experience positive situations and emotions as well by releasing dopamine and serotonin, the two types of neurotransmitters in the brain that are associated with happiness. When you are doing something you love—like dancing or eating a big slice of chocolate cake—your brain recognizes that as a propitious moment, so it releases the chemicals that help you feel good. There are a lot of different positive emotions that people can experience in life such as happiness, excitement, being in love, feeling grateful, joy, peace, and feeling amused. When you are excited, you feel euphoric. When you are doing something that brings you peace, you become more relaxed and content with life. Your stress fades away, and your body goes into a state of calm.

Fostering a positive attitude has always proven to be beneficial to everyone's health. This reminds me of a guy named Greg De Meza. He was an architect in San Francisco, and he was around 56 years old. Greg had been infected with HIV a few years ago, and when he found out, he was in complete shock. It mortified him that at this age in his life when he was supposed to be having fun and living out the rest of his days doing what he loved most, he had to live with this disease that would eventually render him incapable of doing the things he wanted to do. Greg felt stupid and careless. He fell into depression because he regretted the decisions that he had made. He was so embarrassed that he hid his diagnosis from those around him, stopped doing the things he enjoyed, and shut everyone out. Greg was at his lowest point when he finally stopped feeling sorry for himself.

Greg eventually opened up to his friends and family about his HIV status, and he embraced a whole new mindset and attitude toward this disease that was now a permanent part of his life. Greg joined a research program along with 159 other people.

Judith T Mosowitz was a medical social science professor who had conducted a study on this research program where people who were HIV positive were assigned to a training course that would teach them about the five positive emotions. This course helped Greg develop a positive attitude toward his HIV status. He eventually became more optimistic, which led to a significant improvement in his health. It's not rocket science, and you don't have to be a genius to understand how positivity can improve your health.

Speaking Out Words of Positivity

A person who maintains a positive attitude will automatically change how they think, speak, and act. There is a famous saying from the Bible that the power of life and death lies in the tongue, and this couldn't be more true. Speaking out words of positivity over your life will manifest positive results. It doesn't matter if you are not in a positive place in life. What matters is how you think and speak whilst you are in that negative situation. Even if you are facing an incurable illness, one can understand why you would be devastated and depressed, but you don't have to let these negative feelings consume your entire being. You can use the power of positivity to change the quality of your life. It all starts with a simple thought. When you wake up in the morning, instead of thinking about how sick you feel or how hard your day is going to be, try to find something positive to focus on.

Tell yourself that even though you are going through this illness, you are still alive, and you can still spend another day with your family. That is something to celebrate, and you will immediately shift the focus of your thoughts onto something positive. The more positive your thoughts are, the better your overall mood will be. You will smile more often and feel less depressed because you will now be entertaining good thoughts; when you feel good on the inside, it will show on the outside. Speak out words of healing into the universe, say "I am healed," "I am healthy," "I am happy," and you will notice how good you will start feeling.

How Positivity Affects Your Relationships

It's impossible to get through life without building relationships with the people who surround you such as family, friends, teachers, neighbors, and lovers. These relationships could start positively, but somewhere in the middle, they take a negative turn. Family feuds, lovers' quarrels, and fights between best friends are all a normal part of life. People have powerful personalities and opinions that clash, resulting in disagreements. Some family feuds last decades because of the stubbornness and negative attitudes of people involved. Some marriages are on the brink of failure because of the negative words that spouses speak to each other in the heat of the moment. Co-workers brew hate and jealousy against one another because of the negative mindset that they have been nurturing. These issues are a normal part of everyone's lives, but we can turn them around with the help of positivity.

Our Thoughts Affect Our Relationships

You can drastically change your relationships through the power of positive thinking! From your intimate relationships to your casual relationships, you can change the dynamic of any relationship if you just use a positive approach the next time you encounter a disagreement. Are you aware that your feelings, attitude, and actions can affect those around you? What you say, how you say it, and the actions you use all impact the people who are in your life. Can you remember a time when you were having a bad day, and you lashed out at your family or friends without giving a second thought about how it would affect them? The negative emotions you were feeling got the best of you and clouded your ability to think about others before you reacted to a situation. All you desired was to hurt the next person and make them feel the pain that you felt; however, that doesn't do us any good. All it does is add to our regrets list and cause us to feel more guilty at the end of the day.

You are human and things like this will happen. There are so many emotions inside us that it can become difficult to control them when we are upset. When you are having an argument with someone or when your partner has hurt you deeply, the last thought on your mind would be to "think positively." The only thing you would want to do is make that person feel the same pain that they have caused you. This is human nature—to react with anger and negativity when we face a difficult situation. We allow our victim mentality to take over, and we defend ourselves by causing pain to others instead of trying to focus on finding a positive solution to the problem. Sometimes our attitudes and mentality have a lot to do with our upbringing. If we grew up watching our parents reacting to life's struggles with negativity and worry, then we also follow suit and do the same thing as adults.

It's never too late to change this mindset. You can heal your relationships even now by using the right approach, but it won't be easy. If you want to adopt a positive attitude and mindset, it will require you to be the bigger person and put aside your pride. Where there is positivity, pride cannot exist because it instantly causes division and destroys any chance of a resolution. Our thoughts are powerful enough to hinder the growth of something good in our lives. Some people have been in toxic relationships in the past, and when they get into a new relationship with someone else, they destroy that relationship because they allow their negative thoughts and memories to cloud the positive aspects of the current relationship. Focusing on the negative instead of the positive and expecting completely different results is never going to happen. There comes a time when you have to make a choice and stick with it if you want to see a positive change.

Using a Positive Approach

You can change the way you react and respond to a certain situation that arises in your relationships. It's never too late to embrace positivity. Instead of giving in to your desire to get even or to inflict pain on someone else, stop and take a moment to think about how you can react positively. Maybe you can step away from the situation to take some time to cool down before responding negatively. This will help you work through your emotions in a safe space rather than giving in to your carnal desire to strike back. Whoever you are disagreeing with, whether it's your mom, a co-worker, or your partner, you must put yourself in their shoes and try to understand before jumping to conclusions and behaving negatively.

Be slow to anger and quick to understand. Look at the good in the person before you judge them and point out all of their flaws. No one is perfect, and we can all make a lot of mistakes. This is something we all understand well, but this doesn't mean that you should always focus on the bad things that you have noticed about someone. If someone has hurt you, open your mind to the possibility of forgiveness. You don't have to confront that person or continue a relationship with them, but when you forgive them, you are opening yourself up to become more positive by releasing any negative mental attachments. This will start the healing inside you, and eventually, you will also mend the broken relationships that meant so much to you. It is difficult to use a positive approach, and taming the anger and bitterness inside you takes a lot of emotional work, but you can start the process by simply choosing to focus on the positive side of life.

You will draw people closer to you because of your positive attitude. These people will notice a change in your attitude and how peaceful and content you are, when all you could previously do was shout and be angry at everyone and everything. They would want to be around you because of the positive vibes you give off and how you handle your conflicts. A positive person always spreads positivity to those around them, and they are always such a pleasure to be around.

How Positivity Affects Your Career?

Everyone wants to have a successful career, but nobody understands what it takes to become successful. One of the principal ingredients to success is the power of being a positive person with a positive attitude. Whether you're a business owner or you work for someone else, maintaining positivity in everything that you do is extremely important. Businesses face a lot of obstacles that require the strength and optimism of a positive owner and positive staff members to see the business through. Negative thinking people have very limited abilities to find solutions to problems. They cannot think of new ideas that can take the business to higher levels, and they don't know how to react in stressful situations. All they can focus on is how bad everything is getting, and they allow their anxiety and negativity to cut off all chances of survival and growth.

Using Positivity to Improve Your Relationship With Others in the Workplace

There are so many benefits to being a positive thinker in the workplace because it can affect the way you work and how you see yourself as an employee or a business owner. Sometimes people lose sight of how powerful positivity is, and they forget to embrace it, even when it is part of their job. You can enjoy your job and be excited about going to work daily, all you have to do is work on your relationships with your colleagues and your superiors. Let's look at some benefits aside from embracing positivity in the workplace.

Positive Thinking Reduces Stress Levels

When you are facing stressful situations in the workplace, it's challenging to find solutions if you have a negative attitude. As a positive person, you can view these challenges as minor setbacks, and your positivity will equip you to handle them. People who maintain a positive mindset and attitude don't dwell on negative situations, they spend their time focusing on how they can find solutions. When you can solve problems easier, you become happier in your job and less stressed.

You Become More Productive

One of the amazing things about having a positive mind is that you stay stimulated and focused on all the good things. This helps you to be a more productive individual. You have more drive and motivation to pursue challenges and perform better in your job. A negative mindset will hold you back from reaching your full potential, and this will adversely affect your ability to perform at your best. A positive mind is a free mind, and a free mind can see opportunities that others can't.

Your Problem-Solving Skills Improve

Since problem-solving is a skill that few of us possess, it can be even more difficult for people who do not have a positive outlook. When you encounter a problem, the first thing that goes through your mind is how you are going to solve it. People who have a negative mindset cannot see past the issue. All they can see is the situation that they are now stuck in. This way of thinking prevents them from finding a solution, whereas a positive-minded person will shift their focus to see a way out. Positivity will enable you to become creative and solve problems using a positive approach, rather than feeling sorry for yourself and hating your job.

You Gain New Skills

There is no harm in learning all that you can from the surrounding people. Your co-workers all have unique skills. You can take the time to learn from them and broaden your skills base. A positive-minded person would humble themselves and take advantage of the opportunity to learn new skills from others; however, a person with a negative attitude would let pride get in their way of learning from others because they think they are all-knowing or may not care about improving their skills. You can only see the opportunity to grow in all areas of life if you are a positive person.

Receive and Handle Feedback Positively

When your managers or supervisors provide you with feedback on your work performance, it can sometimes be hard to accept if you are taking it the wrong way. But if you have a positive mindset, you would take the feedback as advice and guidance that you can use to improve your performance in your position and at your job. Being able to handle criticism and feedback positively is a cosmic sign of maturity, and it enables you to see the areas where you lack, allowing you to improve on yourself. Negative-minded people are usually stuck in the same place for years because they don't take criticism well, and as a result, they cannot improve themselves. To them, criticism is always a negative thing and may think that they're being scolded or that the person offering the criticism is being harsh. People who have a positive outlook are the ones who move forward in life, constantly improving their skills and bettering themselves.

Improved Conflict Management Skills

Conflict is a sensitive issue that needs to be handled in the best possible way. When a person with a negative attitude faces conflict, they typically blow it out of proportion because they cannot find healthy ways to address it. Conflict is a negative occurrence that needs a positive solution to ensure that it's taken care of. You cannot solve conflict with a negative mindset or approach. As a positive person, you will understand the reason for the conflict, which will immediately allow you to think about solutions. You will see both sides of the conflict, which will help you find a solution that benefits everyone.

In Closing

The importance of positivity cannot go unnoticed. We now understand how crucial it is to our daily lives. Your health, your career, your relationships, and your happiness rely on maintaining a positive mindset. There is nothing to lose by being a positive person. Instead, there is so much to gain from it. Negativity comes easily when you are in a situation that upsets you. It takes a person with a strong will to choose positivity in their thoughts and actions. Make that choice for your life right now. You can go from negative to positive in no time. The five steps that are covered in this book help you kick-start your journey to positivity! You have nothing to lose, so don't be afraid to embrace change and turn a new page into your life. Let's get started on your journey to becoming a positive-minded individual!

CHAPTER 2

Step One—
Face Your Fears Through
Journaling

There is no greater agony than bearing an untold story inside you.

–Maya Angelou

Journal Away Your Stress

Life comes with all kinds of stress and frustrations that affect us daily. Consumed with our busy lives, we don't take the time to sit down and reflect on what happened during our day. Instead, we push our feelings and anxieties aside because we have to focus on other 'important' aspects of life such as work, children, and bills. When you don't take the time to recognize your feelings, you are ignoring your well-being and peace of mind.

Journaling can help you understand your emotions. It is a great way to express your innermost secret feelings. People all around the world use journaling as a coping mechanism to help them plan their day, express their emotions, and find some peace in their busy lives.

The Amazing World of Journaling

Journaling has been around for ages. Some of the most significant people in history have used journals to record their ideas and daily activities. Ludwig Van Beethoven, the great music composer of all time, kept a series of diaries, notebooks, and journals that truly showed who the man behind the music was. This German composer revealed his struggles with deafness and how it drove him to severe depression. He kept his deafness a secret, and this was no simple task for him. He recorded all of his troubles in journals and diaries that he kept safe during the 1770s to 1820s. Marie Curie, the first woman to win a Nobel Prize, recorded her groundbreaking research on radioactivity in her journals. She would spend night and day writing her ideas and recording her progress as she worked toward achieving success. Her journals are now on display at the Bibliotheque Nationale in Paris, where people can view them and get an idea of what was going on inside her mind.

Bringing it back to the modern-day, journals are widely used by people for several reasons, one of the most popular reasons being the ability to express their feelings and get things off their chest. Journaling is a classic way to record your thoughts, experiences, and emotions. Doing this each day helps to ease the burdens that you carry inside your mind, causing a lot of your anxieties and other negative emotions. Some people like to use journaling as a way of reflecting by writing down things from their day to give them a chance to make sense of the situations and give them a chance to evaluate their actions.

The Benefits of Journaling

Journaling has many benefits, and one of the best ones is its ability to decrease stress levels and help keep a logical mind. You wouldn't be able to understand just how effective it is unless you are someone who journals regularly. The incredible effects journaling has on the brain have many scientists amazed, and the benefits have been scientifically proven. Experts at UCLA conducted a study to measure the brain activity of people who journaled. The participants ranged from highly stressed to mildly stressed. Scientists found that people who suffered from intense trauma showed a significant improvement in their brain activity from the amygdala when they started writing about their feelings and experiences (*Benefits of journaling: The science and philosophy behind keeping a diary*, n.d.). When they began putting their experiences into writing, it helped them to process their feelings healthily (*Benefits of journaling: The science and philosophy behind keeping a diary*, n.d.). Let's take a deeper look at how journaling benefits the different areas of your life.

Journaling for Your Immune System

Every time you journal, your brain sheds off the mental load that has been accumulating over the years. All the stress, emotions, and frustration lessen each time you put your feelings into words. This allows your brain to recuperate and breathe a bit. When you are less stressed out, your immune system becomes stronger and more resilient. We use journaling as a stress-relief tool that decreases the stress that causes damage to our immune system. Expressing your inner thoughts and emotions helps keep your mind clear, lowering the risk of you falling prey to various types of illness and diseases. Stress causes several health conditions which render your immune system weak and incapable of fighting back.

Spending at least 20 minutes a day writing about your distress, trauma, and negative emotions can help you lower your chances of getting sick. As you are now aware of the mind-body connection, it should be easier for you to understand how journaling can help keep you healthy, both emotionally and physically. When you bottle up your negative feelings day in and day out, it's like keeping the lid closed on a pressure cooker that is about to reach its limit soon. You do more harm to yourself than good, and this adversely affects your health. Sitting down with a page and pen, letting all of your feelings out onto that page, will bring you so much relief.

Journaling for Your Mental Health

Our mental health is extremely important, and we should give it the same amount of attention as we give to our physical health. As human beings, we face an incredible amount of mental and emotional stress daily. Financial stress, problems with your kids, and disagreements between husband and wife are all common struggles that we face in our lives; however, just because these issues are common doesn't mean that they don't harm the emotional well-being of an individual. When you don't have someone to share your concerns with, your concerns become a heavy weight sitting upon your shoulders. You become caged up in the prison of your mind with nowhere to turn for freedom. This can damage your mental health, causing you to end up with depression and anxiety.

Yes, journaling can bring the much-needed healing that your mind needs, especially when you are looking for a healthy way to cope with your feelings but don't want to go to therapy because you want to learn how to manage your emotions on your own. Diary writing is extremely effective in managing depression. Women who were abused in their relationships use excessive journal writing to help them cope with their feelings of depression. Journaling is like cognitive-behavioral therapy and is quite effective in helping teenagers and adolescents who are at high risk (Ackerman, 2019b).

Journaling for Stress Management

Poor stress management is on the rise among people of all ages today. The increased pressure from life has caused many people to crumble because they don't have a proper system in place to manage their stress. Most people handle their stress by pushing it aside or indulging in substances such as drugs and alcohol to help them blow off some steam; however, this only takes the load off for a little while, and they are back to where they started with even more stress the next day. Using negative coping to help with stress only adds to your current issues because these methods do more harm than good.

Using journaling as a tool to manage your stress yields many benefits that will help you in the long run. You can use a journal to plan out your day by ranging your tasks and responsibilities according to their level of importance. Allow more time for tasks that are difficult to complete and write ways that can help you tackle these tasks more efficiently. Think about what makes these tasks so difficult, and do some research to see how you can use a different approach to help you be more productive. If you are stressed about personal issues, write about what these issues are and what you think can be done to solve them. Brainstorming solutions can help you feel more in control of your problems, and when you feel more in control, there is less to worry about. Journaling provides you with the opportunity to work on improving yourself, so set aside a few minutes each day.

Journaling for Recovery

Whatever trauma, addiction, or illness you are trying to recover from, journaling can help support you on your journey. Part of the healing process is confronting your fears. This can be quite a scary experience, so many people avoid this step when they are on the road to recovery. You cannot truly heal from your trauma or addictions if you do not get to the root of the matter. When you write down your thoughts and emotions and read them back to yourself, you are unknowingly confronting your fears. Journaling plays a vital role in helping you see past the pain so that you can get down to the core of the matter. Below, we have the story of Marie, a 25-year-old who was a survivor of sexual abuse. She explains how she used journaling as a coping mechanism in her life. Let's read on to find out how it has helped her.

Marie's Story

There was a woman named Marie. She was a sexual abuse survivor who used journaling as a way of coping on her road to recovery. Each night, she would lie in bed, unable to sleep because of the flashbacks and horrible memories that played over and over in her mind. Marie needed some sort of outlet, a way to get rid of all that stored fear and anxiety. A friend recommended she try keeping a diary where she could write about all of her experiences. People who have experienced sexual abuse have a hard time opening up to anyone to talk about their experience. There are things they would even hide from their therapist. Marie was one of those people who refused to share everything with her therapist. She buried the intimate details of her trauma deep within her heart because she felt like she couldn't trust anyone enough.

One night, Marie pulled out her diary and started writing how she felt. She was confused about what she should write about first, but after a while, she just closed her eyes and wrote whatever came to her mind. She started writing words like 'pain,' 'sorrow,' 'hopelessness,' 'darkness,' and 'tears.' As she wrote these words, she felt better. Once she got the hang of it, there was no stopping her. Every night before bed, she would share her feelings with her journal. She captured the intimate details of the trauma she experienced. Somehow, the journal gained her trust, and it became a safe place for her to share her troubles. Marie has healed so much just from expressing herself through her journal entries; it gave her someone to rely on, and

she knew her journal would never break her trust, nor would it judge her. Today she has recovered from her trauma and she looks back at her journals to remind herself of how far she has come. The experiences Marie recorded in her journals will serve as a reminder of how much she has survived and pulled through. It will strengthen her and encourage her to move forward in life, no matter what else she may face.

How to Journal Effectively: Tips to Help You Get Started

Journaling can be a bit confusing if you are trying it out for the first time; however, it is fairly simple. The moment you get started, you will notice how beneficial it is and you will become accustomed to journaling daily for your own needs. If you are new to this, don't stress about it. We are here to help you get started. Here are eight easy tips that you can use to start your journey to happy journaling.

You Don't Need Paper to Journal

Although the old-fashioned method of journaling requires a pen and paper, these days you don't need those things if you want to journal. Technology has improved drastically over the years and there are so many new ways that you can journal. If you are a techno-geek, then you would enjoy using digitally based journal applications that can be used on your smartphone, iPad, or laptop. This is a good way of avoiding the extra costs of purchasing diaries and journals regularly since these journal apps have their own online storage cloud where you may save your journal entries as you update them daily. All you have to do to get started is download a journal app that interests you the most, sign up and create an account, and start journaling away.

You Can Write at Any Time of the Day

Some people prefer to journal every morning because it gives them the peace and direction they need to get through the day. Others journal before bed at night because it helps them get stuff off their chest, making it easier to fall asleep. You can journal whenever you want to. There isn't a rule written in stone that you have to journal in the mornings or evenings. Most people have busy lives. From the moment they wake up in the morning until before they go to bed, their life becomes hectic, and it's difficult to find time to journal. Set a time when your environment is quiet and without distractions. This is important because your journaling sessions require your full attention if you want to reap all the benefits.

Join a Support Group

It can be tempting to leave your journey midway and take a break from journaling for a few days; however, days turn into weeks and weeks turn into months. Eventually, your desire to journal fades away and you forget about it altogether. There is a great way to prevent this from happening, and that is to join a support group. Journaling support groups exist for people who are relatively new to this amazing experience. Having that support system around will encourage you to stay committed to the process, and it will also give you some sort of accountability. Communicating with others who are also using journaling to help them cope with trauma, daily stress, or brainstorming, is a great way to stay motivated. Sometimes when you are feeling like you are at a dead end and nothing seems to work, your support group can bring you the positivity you need to come out of that negative space.

Set Your Own Pace and Have Realistic Expectations

When you first start journaling, you don't have to write an entire chapter in one day. Your journal entries should comprise quality, meaningful thoughts, and information. It doesn't matter how many words or pages you write, as long as journaling is helping you achieve a healthy mindset. You can spend 20 minutes on a journaling session and only write one paragraph at the end and it would still be beneficial as long as it helped you. Set your own pace of writing. You don't have to follow what everyone else is doing because your experience is personal and tailored according to your needs. Another important aspect of journaling is that you have realistic expectations and set realistic goals for your progress. You are on a healing journey, and it is crucial that you remain patient with yourself. Everyone heals and grows in their own time, so don't compare yourself to others.

If You Have Nothing to Write About, Use Gratitude

There will be days when you won't have much to write about, but this doesn't mean that you should skip journaling. You can write about anything you want to, whether it's related to your healing or focuses on the things that you are grateful for. Human beings spend so much time focusing on the negative aspects of their lives that they forget to be grateful for all the good things. The only way that we will ever truly be content in life is if we are grateful for the little things. If we can see the importance of the small things in our lives, how much more grateful would we be for the big things? Make gratitude a part of your journaling experience and you will be amazed.

If You Don't See a Change, Try Changing Your Environment

Sometimes people who have journaled for the first time don't see a change in their mindset or their healing. No matter how many sessions they have spent journaling, they still claim to feel the same way as when they first started journaling. A huge reason this could happen is because of the environment they are in during their journaling sessions. Wherever you choose to spend your time is extremely important, as the surrounding environment is powerful enough to affect your mental and physical well-being. For example, you could be a recovering alcoholic who is confident and assured that you won't break your sobriety again; however, being in an environment where there is alcohol around can lead you to become tempted. Fighting temptation can be emotionally draining and this can cause you to backslide in your sobriety.

Similarly, when you are using journaling as a stress management mechanism or as a coping mechanism to help you heal from trauma, you cannot be in a negative environment that reminds you of your pain and trauma. Even if your environment has nothing to do with your pain and trauma, it can still hinder your progress through the noise and other distractions. Consider changing your environment when you are journaling by doing things like getting out of the house to go to a coffee shop for just an hour, sitting in your car alone with the music on, or going to a nearby park where you can be in touch with nature whilst journaling. These minor changes can make a world of a difference, keep this in mind.

Write for Yourself, No One Else

The amazing part about journaling is that you get to write whatever you want, whenever you want, and no one else can see what you have written. Seize this opportunity to write for yourself. You don't have to worry about how neat your handwriting is or whether you have messed up a few pages. When you are writing about your feelings, your handwriting should be able to reflect your emotions. If you have good handwriting, that is fine; however, you don't have to make sure that everything is prim and proper, especially when you are not in the mood. When expressing yourself through your writing, spelling and grammar errors shouldn't be a concern either. As long as you are getting the relief you need when you are journaling, don't worry about anything else. Let nothing hold you back from being brutally honest. Say what you want to say without fear of being judged. It's the only way you are going to benefit from journaling.

Keep a Journal in Your Bag Always

Keeping a journal in your bag for unexpected use is a great idea. Life is unpredictable. If you are recovering from the trauma that you have experienced in your life, having a journal on hand is necessary. Anything could trigger you, causing flashbacks and unpleasant feelings. This is where your journal comes in handy. Being able to write exactly how you are feeling and what caused you to feel like that is a great way to keep track of your healing and to identify potential triggers. It's good to be prepared. You feel more in control of your life when you prepare yourself for unforeseen situations. You can keep a home journal and a work journal, just so that you don't have to stress about remembering to carry it with you every day. If you are using your journal as a coping mechanism to help you overcome your negative feelings, then you have to make sure that you are being responsible and carrying it along with you to work, classes, outings or events, and religious gatherings if you are a religious person.

In Closing

The importance of journaling cannot be overlooked. Even if you weren't a believer in the past, I'm sure that you are one now. The benefits of journaling range from improvements in your mental health to managing your stress more efficiently. In your five-step journey to gaining a healthier mindset, make journaling your number one tool in managing your emotions and tracking your progress. The tips provided to you above help you get started, so put them into practice and start claiming back your life one day at a time. If you want things to change in your life, you have to be the one who changes first. Now that you are aware of what needs to be done to journal effectively, there shouldn't be anything standing in your way of embracing this amazing tool. Remember, you don't need a pen or paper to start. You can access any journal application on your smart device, so cut the excuses and start journaling today!

CHAPTER 3

Step Two—
Dealing With Failure and
Disappointments in a Healthy
Way

Failure is the condiment that gives success its flavor.
–Truman Capote

Learning New Ways to Cope With Failure

Failure is a part of life; just as there is night and day, so too will there be success and failure. The stigma surrounding failure has caused us to perceive it as something to be ashamed of, and people would relate failure to stupidity, laziness, or being incapable; however, there has been a shift in the way people view failure today. We understand it, and it turns out that failure isn't so bad after all. Knowing how to cope with failure and disappointment is vital for your success in life. Having the wrong attitude about it could result in major damage to your self-confidence and motivation. There are ways you can use it to help you deal with disappointments healthily. In this chapter, we will explore this in more detail.

Failures, Disappointments, and Spilled Milk

You must have heard the famous saying, "don't cry over spilled milk." People use this expression when something negative has happened in their lives. It means that you shouldn't spend too much time lamenting over what is lost. Instead, focus on what you still have. That is exactly what we should do whenever we face failures in our lives. Yes, we should express our sadness and regret about what we have failed in; however, we shouldn't entertain any recurrent negative thoughts because they take root in our lives and manifest in other ways.

Failures and disappointments cannot be avoided, but remember that they are just the stepping stones to success. Whether you agree or not, it doesn't change the truth. Try to shift your focus from the negative side of failure to the positive side, and before you question yourself, yes, there is a positive side to failure. People pull away from things they don't understand, and failure is one of the most misunderstood aspects of life. If you had to ask any successful person if they have experienced failure in their lives, their answer would most definitely be a yes. You would never meet a person on this planet who would say that they have never failed at anything in life. Failure is essential in life. There are valid reasons we go through it, yet we don't take the time to think about the lessons that we can learn from failure. Let's look at some reasons behind failure.

Lack of Persistence

Many people fail because they cannot persist in the most difficult of situations. Persistence and resistance are the two most important attributes needed to succeed in life; without them, failure is imminent. When the going gets tough, you cannot crumble under pressure. Instead, remain strong and persevere until the end. Being lazy, unmotivated, or uninterested are reasons you cannot persevere. We go through trials in life so that we may become stronger and rise above our situations. No one said that it was going to be easy. The more you prepare yourself, the better your chances are of pulling through. If you fail repeatedly despite trying your best, maybe your methods aren't working the way you hoped they would. Using the same approach every time will yield the same results. If you want to see a change, use an alternative approach that is outside your comfort zone.

No Conviction

Conviction comes easily to those who understand the importance of right and wrong. When you stand at a crossroads on your journey to success, it's difficult to choose the right path. Temptation arises, and you feel pulled to quit your journey and just give in. If you lack conviction, you will easily give in to temptation, forsaking everything you have worked so hard to achieve. This is how people fail, even after achieving so much success initially. You must be able to convince yourself that you can make it through, despite what you are feeling. Sometimes our feelings get in the way of our ability to see the truth. You must push through this and overcome the urge to ignore what is right in front of you. Conviction is necessary for improving yourself, no matter how much you have messed up. If you want to make a change, you can as long as your desire comes from your heart. Weigh the pros and cons before you decide. The only person you can really trust is yourself, so take the time to think and understand before you decide.

Too Many Excuses

People who encounter failure frequently have a bottomless bag of excuses that they use to justify their reasons for not achieving success in their endeavors. 90% of the time, there is something that prevents them from taking the next step toward their goals.

It is because they are lazy or unbothered. You waste so much time making up excuses and letting them take control of your life, but there will come a time when you have to face your failures and work with them to succeed the next time. Eventually, you will use excuses so much that you even start believing them and lose touch with what is real and what isn't. Failure has reasons, not excuses, and the sooner you understand this, the better it will be for you and your success. Think about how much time you have on this earth. Are you willing to waste it all away on meaningless excuses? Or will you take a stand for your future and take action to overcome your failures?

Blaming Others for Your Mistakes

Failure can devastate some people, and it can cause a lot of emotional stress. When you are experiencing disappointment from failure, it's easy to blame others for your mistakes. In the heat of the moment, you say nasty things and shift the blame onto someone else because you don't want to take responsibility for your actions. Not holding yourself accountable for your own failures can cause you to start developing a pattern where you constantly blame people for all the bad choices you make in your life. You can never break the cycle of failure unless you take responsibility for your actions and decisions. True healing comes from acceptance and acknowledgment of everything you have experienced. You cannot gain closure if you don't accept your faults.

Lack of Discipline

Discipline exists to help us become more responsible in the way we behave and make decisions. When you are disciplined, you are trained to control your emotions and actions so that you can achieve goals or objectives in life. Living life without direction or control leads to a lack of discipline, which always makes it harder for you to make the right decisions. Once you experience failure, there are two choices you have. You can either choose to learn from your mistakes and discipline yourself, or you can behave in the same way and use the same method of getting things done and get the same results each time. Discipline is necessary to help you improve yourself and do better next time so that you will see a change. People these days chose to take the easier way out instead of approaching any situation in a disciplined manner.

Low Self-Esteem

Failing at something in life can have a tremendous impact on your self-confidence. When you don't succeed the first time, it can make you think you are not good enough or smart enough to achieve your goals and dreams. You question your abilities, and when you don't get the answers you are looking for, your self-esteem drops. Now, with zero confidence in yourself, you have no desire to try again, and you eventually lose all hope of succeeding in your goals and dreams. Your self-confidence is the most important factor in achieving your goals. If you don't believe in yourself, you will not see success. Sometimes we listen to the negative voices of others who lie to us because they want to see us fail. This impacts our self-esteem and leaves us questioning our own self-worth. If you cannot see past the lies of people and have faith in yourself, then you are bound to fail. The only voice you should listen to is the voice that motivates you to stay strong on your journey.

Thinking That It's Your Destiny to Fail

In certain instances, when people fail, they put it all on destiny. They believe it was predestined for them to fail and no matter how hard they try, it just won't work out because luck isn't on their side. This type of superstitious thought pattern traps you into believing things that aren't true and it holds you back from pursuing your dreams. There isn't anything wrong with believing in destiny and luck, but when you allow your beliefs to become an obstacle in the path to your success, then you should start second-guessing them. We are all given an equal chance to succeed in life, and our success depends on what choices we make, not on our level of good luck or bad luck.

How to Identify Your Failures and Learn From Your Mistakes

One thing we all can agree on is that it's never easy to accept our faults and failures. Admitting that you made a mistake is one of the hardest things for human beings to do; however, no matter how difficult it is to accept, it is the most important step in learning, growing, and succeeding. The moment you blame other people or destiny for your shortcomings is when you distance yourself from the opportunity to learn from your mistakes. The points mentioned above are signs you can look out for that will help you identify when you are being too dismissive and unreasonable with your failures and mistakes. Learning from your actions is key to change. Here are a few tips to help you accept your failures and learn from them.

Three Things You Need to Learn From Your Mistakes

There are three significant things that need to occur in order for you to learn important life lessons. No one is perfect. We all are bound to make mistakes, but we have to be prepared to follow the process so that we can rise above our failure. Since failure is inevitable, we should spend our time preparing ourselves to rise above the mistakes. The three things you must do are:

- Be willing to place yourself in situations where you will fail and make mistakes.

- Have the self-confidence to take responsibility for your actions and own up to those mistakes.

- Have the courage to try again and make the change that is required for you to succeed the next time around.

There are four different mistakes that people make in their lives, and most people don't even realize that they are making them. Let's look at what these four types of mistakes are in more detail.

Stupid Mistakes

These types of mistakes are the usual idiotic and accidental ones, such as spilling a glass of wine all over your new couch or burning a beautiful pair of pants with a hot iron. Clumsy mistakes are made daily and shouldn't be taken too seriously, although people who suffer from anxiety disorders and other mental health conditions take these mistakes a bit too seriously and it leads to an increase in their anxiety.

Simple Mistakes

Simple mistakes are the type of mistakes that can be avoided; however, people misjudge or overlook a situation that eventually leads to mistakes occurring. For example, not paying your utility bill on time because you forgot and then having your power cut in the middle of you cooking supper. Another example is not planning properly when catering an event, causing you to fall short of cool drinks mid-celebration. These things happen, and they help us judge better the next time around. If you don't make mistakes, how will you learn?

Involved Mistakes

These mistakes are the type that can be understood, but it often takes a lot of effort to prevent them from happening. Arriving late to work every morning because you thought you could leave a little late and get past the traffic, even though you knew that the morning traffic sets you behind at least 20 minutes every day. Knowing that your actions may lead you to commit a mistake and still doing it anyway is known as involved mistakes.

Complex Mistakes

These are the types of mistakes that are so complex that there's no way of avoiding them. Making tough decisions such as whom you should get into a relationship with or which business to invest in are examples of complex decisions. If that business or relationship had to fail because of some unforeseen circumstance, there would be no way of avoiding that, and you wouldn't be able to do anything differently the next time because your actions did not directly cause the failure.

These are the four mistakes that happen in all of our lives, no matter how much we try to avoid them. As much as you might regret making these mistakes, stop and think about why you make them and what lessons you can learn from them. Everything that happens in our lives happens for a reason. We become stronger, wiser, and more resilient with every hardship and failure that we endure. As long as you openly accept your faults and acknowledge your mistakes, you will benefit a great deal from them. Don't know where to start? Worry not! Here's some expert advice to help you focus on the right things that will help you accept your mistakes and learn from them.

Five Ways to Help You Learn Valuable Lessons From Your Mistakes

Every time we make a mistake, we promise ourselves that we will never do it again, but somehow we still repeat that mistake over and over until we finally throw in the towel. The only way you can overcome failure from mistakes is by making the change that is needed to succeed. Change isn't easy. It requires a lot of hard work and perseverance, but it is worth all the sweat and tears that go into it. Below, we have highlighted the important aspects that you should consider on your journey to overcome failure.

Acceptance Is Key

Accepting the good things in life is relatively easy, but accepting the bad things is one of the hardest things anyone could ever do. It takes a lot of courage and wisdom to understand where you went wrong, which is something that few people possess. Being mature about your faults and failures will help you accept them and learn from them. Children usually have a hard time accepting failure because they cannot understand that there is a lesson to be learned from it. Their immaturity prevents them from understanding this, and there are even adults out there who are immature in their mindset, so much so that they cannot see the importance of failure. Allowing yourself to accept the mistakes you make isn't a sign of weakness because it isn't easy to accept fault. Tell yourself, "I made a mistake. I didn't think things through properly." This will help you be honest with yourself and admit to your shortcomings.

Ask Yourself Important Questions

You don't have to dwell on your mistakes, but taking some time to sit down and think about what happened and why it happened will help you understand things. Instead of making yourself upset by thinking of the negative side of things, you should ask yourself a few questions to help you focus on finding out where you went wrong. These are a few examples of the questions you can ask yourself:

- What caused me to fail?

- Could I have prevented this?

  - If so, what could I have done differently?

  - If not, how can I identify future situations like this?

- What lesson did I learn from this?

Make sure that your answers are honest. Write them down in your journal so that you can reflect on the situation. Having things written helps you assess things from a different perspective. Sometimes, you might have everything jumbled up inside your head, but once you put it down on paper, you can track what went wrong and why. Do this when you have time alone. You cannot rush the process or be distracted by outside disturbances.

Plan, Prepare, Persevere

The next step involves planning, preparing, and persevering throughout the learning process. There is no point in beating yourself up over the mistakes or failures you have encountered in the past. Spend your time focusing on ways that you can prepare yourself to do things the right way next time. Planning doesn't happen overnight. Put in the time and effort to ensure that you prepare well. It will not be easy. There will be moments where you become confused, tired, and frustrated, but you must persevere. Giving up is not an option when you are learning from your mistakes. You cannot allow the negative feelings to cripple you. Here are some important tips to remember when planning and preparing for success.

- Leave behind the past and turn a new page. Don't bring yesterday's mistakes into tomorrow's plans.

- Don't look at yourself through the eyes of a failure. Look at yourself as someone with a second chance.

- Make planning a part of your daily routine. Working on yourself should be just as essential as eating and sleeping.

- Write your thoughts and ideas in a journal. This will allow you to track your progress.

If you follow the advice given above, it will surprise you how much you can improve yourself just by planning and preparing using the right methods. It can become difficult to focus and do these things when you are depressed or upset about your failures, so allow yourself some time to get over your feelings before you start this process.

Make It Harder for You to Repeat Those Mistakes

When you have easy access to the tools that helped you make mistakes repeatedly and fail, you are most likely to repeat those mistakes unless you cut off all access to those tools. This reminds me of a story of a lady who developed a shopping addiction because of her loneliness. Every night, she would stay awake late, browsing her shopping apps and buying things she didn't need. She was working on saving money to buy a new apartment; however, all of her extra savings got spent on shopping online. She decided she would not spend any more of her money online, so she came up with a creative way to stop her shopping addiction.

She froze all her bank cards in blocks of ice so that whenever she wanted to buy anything online, she would have to wait for the block of ice to melt to reveal the card details. It would take a while before the ice would melt, giving her enough time to rethink her decision. Think in the same way this lady did, use creative ways to make it harder for you to repeat the same mistakes. Identify what enables you to keep failing at whatever it is you are trying to pursue, and prevent this from happening again.

Find Your Motivation

It's good to identify all the reasons you don't want to fail again.

Think about why you want to succeed so desperately. What are the circumstances behind your desire to make your dreams come true? These factors are the motivation—the driving force behind your willingness to push forward. Everyone is motivated to succeed, so look deep inside yourself to find your motivation. Mothers are motivated by their kids to work hard and stay strong so that they can provide whatever their kids want. Children are motivated to do well in school because of their desire to receive new toys or to eat their favorite ice cream after supper. We are all motivated by something in life, so find your motivation and use it to push forward toward your dreams, no matter how many times you fail.

Dealing With Rejection

We have all experienced rejection in our lives, and although it hurts a lot, it doesn't have to hold you back from living your life. Rejection can come from anywhere. There's no way you can avoid it and no way of telling that it's going to happen. You could be rejected from a job application, rejected by a group of friends, or rejected by the cute guy you had a crush on for the past few weeks. It doesn't matter where it came from, it can still hurt you the same. You put everything on the line, your hopes, your dreams, your heart, and your time, only to be turned down and rejected, and that can cause immense disappointment and pain. Rejection can cause you to lose confidence in yourself, so much so that you never want to try again. When you let rejection hold you back, you miss out on amazing opportunities to succeed in life. Dealing with rejection in unhealthy ways can lead to problems in other areas of your life. Luckily, you can prevent this from happening. These are ways you can deal with rejection the correct way that will enable you to come out even stronger.

Try to Understand Why Rejection Hurts So Much

Everyone needs to be accepted, it's human nature. Acceptance has a lot to do with how we form relationships with other people, so when we are rejected, it makes us feel as if we aren't good enough to be a part of the 'club.' The first step to overcoming rejection is understanding why it is hurting you so much. Were you rejected by a partner? What were the reasons for them rejecting you? Or were you rejected from a job that you applied for? Why weren't you suitable enough for this position? Ask yourself these questions to get a better understanding of whether you really need to work on yourself, or if the rejection was uncalled-for. This will help you decide on what course of action to take next. The more you understand, the better your chances of healing are.

Oftentimes people just get lost in their self-pity after being rejected, they don't stop to think about whether the rejection was valid. You may think, what difference would it make to find this out because the rejection has already happened? Well, you could use this information to work on yourself to prevent this from happening again. Be smart in the way you think, and you will see a change. It's time to open up yourself to learning and growing, instead of wallowing in self-pity and wasting time.

Take a Time Out, and Take Care of Yourself

Amid the shock of being rejected, it's hard to stop and look at yourself. Your mind would be so busy going around in circles, stressing over the why's and the who's, that you would entirely forget to think about your emotional state. Holding back all the anger, shame, and feelings of rejection will only lead to further emotional damage. The best thing you could do for yourself is to take some time away from it all. Take a minor break, just a few days if you can, to work on processing your feelings. Cry if you need to cry. Allow yourself to feel the anger, feel the disappointment, and set yourself free from the negative emotions.

Practicing self-care is also crucial during this time. Rest as much as you can. Your emotions can be draining. Some examples of things you can do to rest your mind and body are to book massage sessions and spa treatments, consider getting a new haircut, go shopping, or just stay in bed and binge on your favorite TV series. Do whatever makes you feel good. That's what self-care is all about. Nursing yourself back to a healthy state of mind is vital for you to move on from rejection. You cannot move on if you are carrying old wounds that you never allowed to heal.

Spend Time With the People You Love

There is no better way of overcoming rejection than spending time with the people who love and accept you. When you are dealing with rejection, your family and friends can remind you how special you are to them. Taking your kids out for a fun day at the movies or going on a date with your significant other are ways you can remind yourself just how important you are to your family. Can you think back to a time when you were rejected for whatever reason? Did you feel unwanted and unappreciated? Did you think that there was something wrong with you, or maybe you didn't have what they were looking for? Were you left questioning your self-worth and abilities? And you felt like possibly others felt the same way, but they didn't know how to tell you?

I'm sure you answered yes to these questions because that's what rejection does to us all. It leaves you second-guessing yourself and your relationships with those around you, and it plants seeds of doubt into your mind. Don't let these seeds grow. Destroy all your doubts by surrounding yourself with the people who love you.

Develop Healthy Habits

Being emotionally frustrated and stressed can cause you to become involved in developing unhealthy habits such as drinking alcohol, smoking cigarettes, and possibly even doing drugs. These quick fixes help to mask the pain you are feeling, but they don't offer a long-term solution. In fact, these bad habits are addictive and can have deadly side effects on the brain and the body. You can prevent this from happening by engaging in good habits instead of the bad. Here are a few good habits you can indulge in to help you recover from rejection.

Eat Healthy and Drink Lots of Water

Eating healthy foods such as fruit and vegetables and foods that are low in fat, sugar, and carbs are beneficial for your mind and your body. The fewer toxins you put into your system, the healthier you will feel. When people are depressed, they often crave comfort foods like chocolates, ice cream, cakes, and soda drinks. Whatever tastes good makes you feel good. That is why people turn to junk food to overcome their sadness; however, junk foods fill your body with sugar and unwanted carbs, which leave you feeling sluggish, bloated, and exhausted both mentally and physically. Healthy foods boost your energy, keep your mind clear, and help your body function well. Drinking lots of water is also essential for a rational mind and healthy body. Water flushes out toxins from your body, which are also caused by stress. When you stress, harmful toxins build up in your body, causing health conditions such as heart disease, headaches, digestion problems, and fatigue. Avoid drinking alcohol frequently, and cut down on smoking if you are already a smoker.

Exercise Regularly

Part of keeping yourself fit involves exercising and other forms of physical movement such as yoga and dancing. Some people prefer spending a power hour at the gym, while others prefer practicing yoga in the comfort of their own homes. To each their own, as long as it helps you get your blood pumping and muscles moving. Dancing can also be used to exercise and keep fit as well. There are various forms of dancing that help you express your emotions and keep healthy at the same time. You can start small by spending just 10 minutes a day exercising. You can go for a brisk morning walk or jog in the evenings when you get home from work. There are so many options available for your preference, so try your best to make exercise a regular part of your life.

Get Enough Sleep

Sleep is such an important aspect of our lives as human beings, yet so many people underestimate the power of sleep. People overwork themselves, spending days, and even nights, focusing on their jobs. They neglect their health and deprive their bodies of much-needed rest that's needed to function normally. Lack of sleep can affect your mental health and emotional well-being, pushing you deeper into depression. Train your body to be in bed by 9:30 p.m. at the latest so that you can get a good night's sleep of at least seven hours. A well-rested mind and body make clearer decisions and work more responsibly.

In Closing

One thing is for certain: as long as you are a human being, you are bound to make mistakes. You were not born perfect. There will be things you won't be good at, and the only way you will know this is by trying first. Don't be too hard on yourself if you discover you cannot succeed at something. If you feel it isn't for you, move on to something that you see yourself succeeding in. Listen to your heart and follow your dreams. You don't have to do what someone else tells you to do. Success and failure are a natural part of life, accepting that is the first step toward learning from your mistakes. There is no shame in failure, and don't let anyone tell you otherwise. Failure is there to make you a stronger, wiser, and more determined person. Your failures don't define who you are as a person. How you rise above it is what determines your personality and ability. It's time that you let loose and stop trying to control everything in life. In the next chapter, we look at how the constant need for control consumes your life and makes you miss out on the opportunity to live life the way it was intended.

CHAPTER 4

Step Three— Don't Be a Control Freak

Life is to be lived, not controlled; and humanity is won by continuing to play in the face of certain defeat.
–Ralph Ellison

Learn to Let Loose and Live

People these days are consumed with the desire to be in control of every aspect of their lives. Having control over your career, your love life, your kids, and your home is good. It's necessary to maintain a certain amount of control in the important areas of life; however, being too controlling can cause you to develop a great dissatisfaction over your life. Life should be enjoyed, yes there will be moments where you will face difficulties, but no matter how much control you have, there will still be problems and trials that come up. Understanding the dark side of control is essential, especially when you no longer enjoy your life unless you control every aspect.

Are You a Control Freak?

Having the ability to identify whether you are a control freak is something few people can do because they are unaware of the signs. If you find yourself in the same boat, take our quiz to help you find out just how controlling you are. Answer the following questions truthfully so that you will receive an accurate result on the quiz.

I like to plan and micromanage every aspect of my life.

a) Never

b) Rarely

c) Sometimes

d) Always

I don't enjoy asking for help, and I don't take help from others.

a) Never

b) Rarely

c) Sometimes

d) Always

I prefer to spend a lot of my time organizing my surroundings and keeping everything in place.

a) Never

b) Rarely

c) Sometimes

d) Always

Whenever I deviate from my daily routine or rituals, I become very upset and irritated.

a) Never

b) Rarely

c) Sometimes

d) Always

I have trouble admitting to my mistakes or accepting blame when I am wrong.

a) Never

b) Rarely

   c) Sometimes

   d) Always

I think I work better alone, rather than in a team.

   a) Never

   b) Rarely

   c) Sometimes

   d) Always

I find it hard to apologize to people that I may have hurt.

   a) Never

   b) Rarely

   c) Sometimes

   d) Always

I like everything I do to be perfect, or I just won't do it at all.

   a) Never

   b) Rarely

c) Sometimes

d) Always

I don't enjoy living with disorganized people.

a) Never

b) Rarely

c) Sometimes

d) Always

I spend a lot of time worrying about the things I can't control.

a) Never

b) Rarely

c) Sometimes

d) Always

Results

Rarely or Never

If your answers were mostly between never and rarely, then you have nothing to worry about. You are as cool as a cucumber, and you enjoy minding your own business. You let go of things you can't control and you never obsess over the past, present, or future. Whether it's your home, job, or interests, you maintain a decent amount of control over them, and you never go beyond what is necessary. You easily click with others, and you don't enjoy sticking your nose in their business. When faced with rejection, you quickly adapt to the situation without feeling like you lost control. You can admit to your mistakes, and you accept blame when you mess up. All in all, you do not have a controlling personality; instead, you are easy-going and carefree.

Sometimes or Always

If your answers were mostly within the range of sometimes and always, then I hate to break it to you, but you are a control freak! Having the urge to be in control of everything around you is a cosmic sign that you may be someone who has a controlling personality. Now that you are aware of your controlling issues, it would be a good idea to make a change as soon as you can. You deserve to enjoy your life without having to stress about every little detail.

Why Do People Crave Control?

Let's be honest, we all want to be in control of our lives. We want to feel empowered and liberated in every aspect of life because when you don't have control, you become vulnerable, and that scares all of us. No one likes to be in a position where they are being controlled by someone or something else. The thought of dancing to the music of someone else, following their every word and not having any backbone to stand up for yourself is a terrifying way to live. And that alone is reason enough to want to have complete control over your life. Each one of us is so different. We live different lives; we have distinct personalities, and we come from different backgrounds, but we all share similar goals and dreams—to be successful, to have a family, to own a home and so much more. We also understand that the only way to achieve our goals is to be in control at all times.

While this is true to a certain extent, there is no guarantee that you will find success in all you do just because you have control. Anyone can lose the plot suddenly, no matter how much control they have. Life takes unexpected turns. There's no way you can predict where life is going to take you, so you just need to experience what life offers. People who don't understand this basic principle have a hard time letting go of things they can't control. Every single person in this world has basic needs that have to be fulfilled in order for us to survive; things like food, shelter, sleep, clothing, love, intimacy, employment, safety, esteem, and recognition. And when we feel like we don't have control, we fear these needs won't be met, so we turn into control freaks so that we can ensure that these needs are met.

How Does Being Controlling Impact Your Life?

There are many downsides to being a controlling person, many of which involve becoming isolated. Have you ever noticed how a person with a controlling personality behaves? You would agree with me when I say that they seem like the least fun people to be around. Of course, it would be annoying to spend time with them because they would be in a constant state of stress due to all the different things they had to control. Honestly speaking, who would have time for fun if they were busy being control freaks? Apart from that, there are several disadvantages that come with wanting complete control. We have mentioned a few of them below.

Constantly Stressed and Frustrated

If you want to be in control of everything, then you must also be prepared to deal with the increased amount of stress that comes with the responsibilities. The reason you desire to control everything is because you have a certain way that you prefer things to be done and believe that you are the only one that can get them done perfectly, and when things don't go as planned, it causes a tremendous amount of stress and frustration. You constantly think about everything you have to take care of because you want to make sure that you have it all planned out well in your mind so that you don't miss out on important details.

No Room for Fun

People who have controlling personalities find it next to impossible to have fun and let loose. There is a fear of losing control that looms over them, making it difficult to enjoy anything. Putting yourself in a position to have fun means that you are going to be vulnerable, and this can be scary for most people who crave control. Can you imagine living life without enjoying all the significant moments? Hanging out with friends, going to parties, spending the weekend away, or just taking a few days off to lie in bed and relax. This might sound enticing to those who don't have a problem with control, but for others, this might sound terrifying because it would mean that they would have to relinquish their control in order to have fun.

Decrease in Your Social Life

No one enjoys being around people who have a controlling personality, mainly because they always want things to go their way, and they never accept fault when they make a mistake. The secret to a successful friendship is being able to compromise and help each other out when necessary; however, people who like to be in control cannot maintain friendships because they can never compromise or accept help from anyone else. They have the need to constantly be right, even when they are wrong, and they cannot see eye to eye with another person. People avoid you, they don't invite you to their events, and they pull away from socializing with you altogether.

Increased Risk of Developing Mental Health Issues

People who have controlling personalities are more at risk for developing mental health issues such as anxiety disorders and depression. The constant stress and pressure that you experience from trying to control everything affects your state of mind and causes you to become mentally exhausted. When your mind cannot cope with high levels of stress, it reacts with the fight-or-flight response. Soon, you develop anxiety disorders, which can become severe quickly if not addressed in time. As time goes by, you become more susceptible to various other mental health conditions; however, you can prevent that from happening by allowing yourself to step back and relax.

When Would It Be Beneficial to Have Complete Control?

For those people who have always had a bit of a controlling side, here's some good news for you. It turns out that being a bit of a control freak might actually benefit you in certain situations.

Knowing when to exert your control is very important. You must know your surroundings and understand the people with whom you engage with daily. Sometimes control is necessary. Without it, things would simply fall apart. Let's look at the various situations where control would be a good thing.

Controlling Your Actions

Somehow, we all lose control from time to time. Unforeseen circumstances occur suddenly, placing you in a difficult position where your reaction might not be as calculated as you'd expect. Imagine you're out shopping with your family. Everyone is having fun and enjoying each other's company. You all decide to visit a certain restaurant for supper, unaware of the calamity that is about to occur. The server seats you and your family at one table outside, where it is cool and breezy. Suddenly, a disagreement occurs between you and another person from the neighboring table. The issue quickly escalates, and you eventually reach your limit. As much as you want to slap that person across the face, you restrain yourself because you prefer not to worsen the situation. That is how you control your actions. Most people wouldn't have hesitated to react violently. It takes a disciplined individual to hold back their fists.

Controlling Your Emotions

Emotional control is essential to help us succeed in all areas of our lives. We face all kinds of situations daily, most of which cause us to become stressed; however, in order for us to get through the day, we have to control our emotions and focus on what needs to be done. Sensitive people have a hard time focusing once they are exposed to situations that make them emotional. Mastering emotional control is important for sensitive people because it can help them overcome and conquer any trial. A person who cannot control their emotions becomes vulnerable to being judged by others. People watch how you handle situations and how you react to conflict. The ability to control your emotions says a lot about your maturity and professionalism, therefore, it is crucial that you always keep your feelings in check, and handle difficult situations without being influenced by your emotions.

Controlling Your Time

Time goes by so quickly, especially when you are doing things you enjoy. In today's busy world, people's days are filled with several significant tasks and responsibilities. There isn't enough time to do the things you want to do, such as spending time with your loved ones or relaxing after a long day. Without proper time management, things can become even more hectic for you and you would miss out on so much more. Being in control of your time is essential. In your career, there would be deadlines you have to meet, and in your home life, there would be special moments you don't want to miss like tucking the kids in for bed or having supper as a family. Controlling how much of your time you spend doing certain tasks will allow you to stick to a routine and make time for what's important as well.

Controlling Your Finances

Money is a sensitive topic for many people. Not everyone can afford to live a comfortable lifestyle like the rich and famous. With your finances, maintaining control is vital. You must be able to budget yourself and work with what you have. A little can go a long way if you know how to control your money. Being lavish and spending without thinking about tomorrow is never a good choice. It doesn't matter if you are a millionaire or working for minimum wage, having control over what you spend your money on is a good way of tracking your finances. Control is good in this area of life, as it helps you to be more responsible and aware of how you spend your money. Losing control or being too lenient could cost you your future.

How to Stop Being So Controlling in Life

After spending years being a full-on control freak, it will be hard to simply give everything up and stop exerting control. Change involves a process, and nothing happens overnight. You have to first prepare your mind for the change that is going to take place, otherwise, it would be even more difficult to make the change a reality. It all starts with the mind. Once you have decided about doing something, you know you will see it through. Understand that it will not be easy. There will be times when you feel like nothing will ever change. Retraining your mind and actions takes a lot of work, so be easy on yourself and don't expect results too soon. The more you work on yourself, the more change you will see. Below, we have provided some advice on how you can start letting go of the things you can't control, and how you can accept the uncertainties of the future. But first, here are some signs that you can look out for that show you are a control freak.

Signs That Show You Are a Control Freak

Sometimes the signs can be so clear in front of us, yet we turn away and remain in denial because we don't want to accept the truth; however, if you are ready to make a change, you have to first accept that you have a controlling personality. Without acknowledging the problem, there cannot be any solution. Here are signs that you have a controlling personality. Be honest and open about whether you see these signs in yourself.

- You prefer to live a life where you can easily predict what is going to happen next, and you follow a set routine that has worked well for you over past years. When something happens unexpectedly, it causes you to divert from your routine and you become anxious and upset over it.

- You are very organized, and you like to follow a system to get things done.

- When you are planning an event and things don't go your way, you become frustrated and anxious because your vision isn't being reached.

- The standards you set for yourself and others are extremely high.

- You are stuck in a one-way type of thinking, where you see only one way to get something done right, and you refuse to try new ways.

- You prefer to do things by yourself, instead of asking anyone for help.

- You find it hard to relax and let go after a long day. Even when you are on vacation, you cannot seem to have fun or keep your mind free from worry.

If you notice any of these signs in yourself, chances are that you could be a control freak. Once you have acknowledged this and are ready to make a change, the next step would involve retraining your mind and your actions. Here are some tips below to help you make the change.

Tips to Help You Stop Being So Controlling

The road to change is never easy, but if you stay committed, you will reach your goals. Whenever you feel like giving up, remember how frustrating and exhausting it is to constantly be in control of everything around you. Think about how much more peaceful your life can get once you stop being so controlling. It's worth all the work you put into the process. Soon you will become more relaxed, outgoing, and open to the idea of having fun. Get ready for a change!

Be Aware of Your Thoughts and Actions

Being aware of your controlling thoughts and actions is the most important part of the process. Journaling can benefit you a great deal by helping you keep track of your thoughts. Whenever you notice any controlling thoughts or behaviors, write them down in your journal. This will help you identify situations where you become more controlling, and it will bring awareness to your secret thoughts, which fuels your desire to control.

Understand Your Feelings

If you want to change your controlling behavior, understand

what is causing you to behave that way. Your feelings can push you to the edge, especially when you are a controlling person who is constantly anxious about making sure that everything goes as planned. Take some time each day to sit alone and ask yourself a few questions to help you understand. "What is causing you to fear so much?" "Why do you have to always be in control of everything?" These are some questions that you can ask. When you are feeling emotional, your mind focuses on a million different things, causing you to stress and become overwhelmed. Fearing the unknown causes anxiety and pushes you to become more controlling.

Reroute Your Thoughts

Now that you have identified thoughts that bring out the fear and anxiety in you, you can replace them with calmer, more positive thoughts that help to keep you grounded. If you cannot identify fear-based thoughts, how will you change them? Keep an eye out for these intrusive thoughts that cause you to fear. Here's what they sound like.

- "If we don't leave early for the Christmas party, the entire event will be ruined."

- "I have to finish this book before Monday or else my book club members would kick me out."

- "Driving to work every day is going to ruin my car. I have to find a different mode of transport."

These are the thoughts that enter your mind suddenly, instilling fear and anxiety in you. As soon as you notice these kinds of thoughts forming, shift your focus onto the positive side of things. Ask yourself how sure you are that this would happen. Do you have any evidence to back up your thoughts? Is this way of thinking helpful to you? Do you think maybe your emotions are clouding your judgments? These questions will help you counter your negative thoughts and eliminate them before they instill fear in you.

Learn to Accept That Not Everything Is Going to Be In Your Control

No one can control everything in life. If this was possible, imagine how boring our lives would be. Every day you would know exactly what you were going to do, you'd know what to expect, and everything would go your way. Fortunately, this is not the case in reality. There are many things in life that we have no control over, and we need to accept this if we want to live fulfilling lives. Choosing to accept the things we can't control gives us the freedom to live the way we want to. Spend some time thinking about all the things you find hard to control. Do these things have to be controlled by you? Can they function on their own or with the help of someone else? If you are not needed, learn to accept that and let go of these situations. You will become so much happier and more relaxed after you stop stressing about things that are out of your control.

Understand That You Are Not Perfect

Perfection exists among the non-living. As human beings, there is no way that we are considered perfect individuals. We make mistakes and mess up in life, and there isn't anything wrong with that. Society has molded us into thinking that mistakes are bad or that they mean you are not good enough. So when you make a mistake, they instantly judge you as someone who doesn't have it all figured out. Who said human beings have to be perfect? Where did we get the idea that our mistakes define us as a person? You understand that you are not perfect, no one is. We all have our own special way of dealing with things. When you realize that you are not perfect, you will loosen your grip on certain things that you can't control. Other people are not perfect either, so if they cannot get something done in the same way as you want, accept that and move on without getting upset.

Change Can Also Be Good

Not all change is bad. There are certain instances where change can be one of the best things that could happen to you. Sometimes people fear change because of unpleasant experiences they have encountered in the past, so when they go through changes in the future, they become anxious and defensive toward it. This leads them to tighten their control so that they can try to avoid a change in their lives. The more fear they feel, the more in control of their lives they want to be. Your life can never stay the same forever. We all change and strengthen at different stages in our lives, and this requires us to embrace the change with open arms. This can be extremely difficult, especially when people don't understand why the change is taking place. Educate yourself, seek to understand first before you jump to conclusions and expect the worst. Not everything is as it seems. It can surprise you at any moment in life. That is why it is so important that we learn to adapt to change fast because, these days, life is changing so often, and we don't control the events that are taking place. All we can do is go with the flow and hope for the best. Covid-19 came as an unexpected shock that shook the entire world to its core. No one was prepared for what was to come, and people had a hard time accepting this change. Eventually, we all had to adapt to it and let go of the things we couldn't control.

In Closing

Our controlling personalities make it impossible for us to

achieve a clear mindset or develop a positive attitude. With all the stressful thoughts and impulsive reactions, your brain would have become accustomed to functioning in this manner. Break the chains of your controlling ways if you want to live a stress-free life. A positive mindset starts with the wisdom to understand negative thoughts. Focus all of your energy and time on something more important, such as working toward a healthy mindset, rather than spending your time worrying about things you can't control. The sooner you accept life for what it is, the better you will be at adapting to sudden change.

CHAPTER 5

Step Four—
Breathing and Meditation to Help
You Achieve a Healthy Mind and
Body

A healthy body leads to a healthy mind.
—Pooja Agnihotri

How Does Breathing Exercises and Meditation Benefit You?

Many people use different breathing exercises to help them overcome stress and anxiety. You don't have to pop a lot of prescription pills just to help calm down your stressed and paranoid mind. There are healthier options to choose from such as meditation, yoga, breathing exercises, and other forms of sports. If you haven't tried out any of these options yet, it would be difficult for you to see how it would benefit you. In this chapter, you will learn all about breathing exercises and meditation, and we will explain the different exercises to choose from.

The Importance of Breathing Exercises

Breathing exercises can transform your life, helping to eliminate stress and worry. It can alter the way you think and how you process your feelings. A simple breath goes a long way, and people don't understand the benefits that come with practicing breathing exercises regularly. To understand its benefits, you have to first understand the science behind breathing. There is a lot you are unaware of for breathing and how it works. Let's explore this amazing science in more detail below.

The Science Behind Breathing Exercises

There are many important educational institutions and government organizations, all of which boast the importance and benefits of breathing exercise to reduce stress and treat depression and anxiety. The respiratory system consists of:

- Nose (nasal cavity)

- Pharynx

- Larynx

- Trachea

- Bronchi and bronchioles

The nose brings air into your body, and it is filled with tiny hairs that sterilize the air before it passes into your lungs. There are different respiratory muscles that help transport air down into your lungs and back again and they are the diaphragm, the rib cage muscles, and the abdominal muscles. All the different organs in your body need fresh air to function because your blood transports oxygen to your organs from your bloodstream. Whenever you take deep breaths in and exhale after a little while, you will feel much less stressed and more energized. Breathing in through your nose and breathing out from your mouth is the most common way to perform breathing exercises. As the air travels into your nose, it is carried to your lungs and absorbed into the bloodstream, where it is taken to all different areas of your body. This new oxygen helps to eliminate any stress hormones in the blood, which calms you down and helps you think clearly. Therefore, breathing exercises are so important because they work so effectively in reducing stress levels instantly.

How Does Breathing Exercises Benefit You?

Breathing is our basic method of survival. Without it, we would all cease to exist. There are many benefits of breathing exercises, especially if you are an active person. You can use these exercises to help you combat difficult situations when your anxiety gets the better of you. Here are some examples of the benefits of breathing exercises.

Significantly Decreases the Toxicity of the Body

Your body quickly becomes acidic due to all the stress, junk food, and exhaustion that you expose yourself to. The effects of stress often go unnoticed by people. Day by day, we continue to ignore the signs that our body sends our way. The body develops toxins when exposed to high levels of stress and anxiety. These toxins build up in our bodies and cause different complications to our health. You can free your body from these toxins by reducing your anxiety and stress symptoms using deep breathing techniques.

Improves Your Sleep

Leading a stressful lifestyle can cause many issues which affect your sleep. Overthinking at night, increased anxiety, insomnia, and other disorders play an enormous factor in why you cannot get a proper night's rest. When your mind is chaotic, there is no way you will sleep. Sleep is essential for us to perform at our best every day. Your mind and body will shut down if it doesn't rest when needed, and this will impact all areas of your life. Breathing exercises help improve your sleep by calming your mind and removing all the chaos.

Reduces Anxiety

Anxiety is harmless when experienced in small amounts now and then; however, when your anxiety takes over your life, it becomes an obstacle to your success, and it holds you back from taking chances and putting yourself out there. There are so many types of anxiety disorders that exist today, and most of the time, they cannot be identified without the help of a professional. One of the effective ways of dealing with anxiety is through breathing exercises. When you engage in slow breathing exercises, you allow your mind to slow down and make sense of everything that is happening in life. Living in a constant state of anxiety and fear can be exhausting, luckily you have an immediate technique to help you get rid of all the anxiety, which is the breathing exercises.

Improves Digestion

Digestion issues are common among people nowadays, from irritable bowel syndrome (IBS) to gastrointestinal problems. These digestive issues can affect the quality of your life significantly. Deep breathing exercises can help improve your digestion issues by increasing the amount of oxygen in your digestive system. This helps to move things along well and gets the intestines working properly. Stress can also play a part in causing issues with your digestive system, so the breathing exercises will also help to eliminate stress, thus correcting the concern.

Eliminates Negative Thoughts

Negative thoughts easily enter our minds without warning, causing undue stress and frustration. When these thoughts play on repeat in our head, it becomes too much to handle, and we eventually become vulnerable to depression and anxiety. You can use breathing exercises to help you eliminate the negative thoughts one by one. When your mind is clear, it gives you the ability to identify negativity in any situation; however, when your mind is chaotic, negativity will pass through undetected. Meditation and breathing exercises go hand in hand to help you combat negative thoughts and behaviors.

Top 10 Breathing Exercises You Can Use

There are many types of breathing exercises that exist today, but there are only a select few that actually make a difference to your mind and body. Not everyone is the same. Different exercises will work best for different people. It depends on your preference, your abilities, and your reasons for doing these exercises. We are exploring breathing exercises to help you get rid of stress and negativity from your mind and body. The exercises, highlighted below, are great for improving your mind and encouraging positivity. You can try them all and stick with the ones that make the most difference to your state of mind.

Alternate Nostril Breathing Exercise

This type of breathing exercise is also known as "nadi shodhana," and it involves breathing through each nostril alternatively. You perform this exercise by blocking off one nostril and breathing in through the other and vice versa in a pattern. It is best to carry out this exercise in a seated position instead of standing up or laying down. This exercise helps to relieve anxiety in the mind and body. Here are the steps to follow to do this exercise correctly.

- You will start by positioning your right hand in the Vishnu Mudra position, which involves bending your index finger and your pointer finger toward your inner palm. Leave your thumb, ring finger, and pinky finger open and extended outward.

- Next, you can choose to either close your eyes or gaze downward softly.

- Block off your right nostril using your thumb.

- Inhale deeply through your left nostril and then exhale slowly.

- Next, block off your left nostril with your ring finger.

- Inhale deeply through your right nostril and then exhale slowly.

- Repeat as many times as you require.

Try to do at least 10 reps of this breathing exercise each day. Please note that if this is your first time doing this exercise, you might feel light-headed. If this is the case, take a break and drink some water. You can resume the exercise when you feel normal again.

Belly Breathing Exercises

The American Institute of Stress suggests that 20 to 30 minutes a day of deep belly breathing exercises will reduce stress significantly (Ankrom, 2021). You will need to find a comfortable place to perform this exercise. There shouldn't be any noise or disturbances around you. You can choose to sit on a comfortable chair or lie down on the bed with a pillow under your head and your knees, or you could sit cross-legged on the floor. This type of exercise helps strengthen your diaphragm, which is the muscle responsible for helping you breathe. Once you find a good place to perform this exercise, follow the steps below to get started.

- Place one hand on your tummy, below your rib cage, and place your other hand lightly on your chest.

- Your belly should be relaxed. Don't force it or squeeze it inward by tightening your core muscles.

- Inhale slowly through your nose. You should be able to feel your tummy rising slowly, your hand along with it, as you breathe in.

- Purse your lips slightly and exhale through your mouth. Pay attention to your hand that is resting on your chest. It should remain in the same position.

- Repeat as many times as you wish.

This type of belly breathing exercise aims to make you aware of your breath movements and how it influences your body. The rising and falling of your belly as you inhale shows you that fresh oxygen is being carried throughout your body whenever you breathe. When you exhale, you will see how your belly and chest move inward as the carbon dioxide leaves your body. In with the good and out with the bad. This breathing exercise will teach you how to take in what is good for you and let go of what isn't right for you.

4-7-8 Breathing Exercise

The 4-7-8 breathing exercise, also known as the relaxing breath exercise, helps to relax your mind and body, and it acts as an all-natural tranquilizer for the central nervous system. When you first start practicing this exercise, you should sit upright with your back against the wall; however, once you become accustomed to it, you can perform the exercise whilst lying down. Here are the steps to follow.

- To start this exercise, you must first place the tip of your tongue behind the upper part of your front teeth, where you feel the tissue of your gums. It should remain there throughout the duration of the exercise.

- Next, exhale through your mouth, whilst making a *whoosh* sound.

- Close your mouth and count to four in your mind. As you do this, inhale slowly through your nose.

- Hold your breath for seven seconds.

- Exhale through your mouth once again, making a *whoosh*

sound whilst counting to eight.

This exercise will help you relax and calm down your nerves. As you repeat the exercise, you will notice how much more calm and focused you become. This exercise is great for people who suffer from anxiety, depression, and other mental health disorders where they are always stressed and on edge. The best thing about this exercise is that you can even do it whilst lying in bed so that it can help you fall asleep.

The Lion's Breath

The lion's breath, also known as 'simhasana' in Sanskrit, is a powerful breathing exercise that helps you relax your facial muscles, especially around your jaw. It can ease anxiety and stress and improve your cardiovascular functions. During this exercise, you will be required to roar like a lion while sticking out your tongue. You will need a quiet, comfortable place to practice this exercise. Here's how you perform this exercise.

- Be seated in a slightly leaning forward position with your hands on your knees or on the floor.

- Next, inhale deeply through your nose.

- Open up your mouth wide as you stick out your tongue, stretching it down toward the top of your chin.

- Exhale sharply and forcefully. Make sure that your breath moves from the start of your tongue to the end.

- Make a *haa* sound as you exhale. It should be carried from deep within your tummy.

- Take a brief break and breathe normally for a few minutes.

- Then repeat the lion's breath exercise as many times as you wish.

Initially, this exercise would seem like a waste of time. By the looks of it, you would think that it's all made up. But when you do it, you will slowly notice the change in your stress and anxiety levels. Stick to the process and don't let your doubts get the better of you.

Mindful Breathing

Mindful breathing is a great breathing exercise that also includes mindful meditation. In this exercise, you must pay attention to your breathing and focus on what is happening in the present. Your mind should not be allowed to drift off to the past or the future. Once again, you will need to find a quiet place to perform this exercise, as distractions could shift your focus. Here's what you should do next.

- You must choose something calm to focus on, a calming phrase like "breathe in peace, breathe out negativity" or choose a focus word like 'love' or 'light.' These words will be the focal points that you will use during this exercise.

- As you inhale, think about the focus word you have chosen, and as you exhale, allow the negativity to leave your body.

- Let go of all the stress and tension. Close your eyes and repeat the exercise as many times as you need. You'll notice that your mind slowly drifts off. Once this happens, bring it back to the present.

Mindfulness breathing will help you focus on the issues at hand, not on the things of that past which you cannot change. Your awareness has to be on point during this exercise. You cannot be tired or distracted when you are doing this or else there would be a lot of mistakes made.

Pursed-Lip Breathing Exercise

This type of breathing exercise will help you become relaxed and stress-free by intentionally slowing down your breathing. Pursed-lip breathing is a simple breathing exercise that many people use daily; some people use it to help them combat negative emotions, and some people who suffer from lung-related health conditions such as emphysema and chronic obstructive pulmonary disease (COPD) may use it to help maintain or strengthen their lungs. Here are the steps you can use to do this exercise.

- Make yourself comfortable, and sit in a position with your neck and shoulders relaxed. Don't be tense or stiff.

- Inhale slowly through your nostrils. Make sure that your mouth is closed when you are inhaling.

- Next, exhale through your mouth, pucker up your lips, and count to four as you do so.

- Maintain a slow and steady pace when you are exhaling. Feel the air leaving your mouth.

Consider practicing this breathing exercise around three to four times a day. You can practice while you are at work, during your breaks, at night before you go to bed, or even while you are taking a shower. You will eventually master the art of pursed-lip breathing exercises.

Resonance Breathing Exercise

Also known as coherent breathing, resonance breathing is a type of exercise that can help put you in a relaxed state. It helps keep your anxiety and fears at bay, and it's relatively easy to perform. Here are the steps.

- Lie down on the floor or on your bed, whichever you prefer.

- Breathe in through your nose gently, keeping your mouth closed. You don't have to rush or fill up your lungs with too much air. A simple, deep breath is good enough. Count to six as you are inhaling.

- Exhale slowly, count to six again as you are exhaling. Let the air leave your body slowly. Don't force it.

- Repeat the exercise for a minimum of 10 minutes. You can add more time if you want to.

- Take that time to focus on yourself and understand how your body feels.

Sitali Breathing

This type of breathing exercise is also practiced in yoga. The main purpose behind this exercise is to lower your body temperature and calm your mind. You will be required to breathe in through your mouth a lot, so find a clean place that is free from dust to conduct this exercise. Here are the steps you have to follow to do this exercise.

- Be seated in a comfortable position.

- You must stick out your tongue and curl it inward to bring the edges together. If you cannot achieve this, you can use the pursed-lip position instead.

- You will inhale through your mouth, keeping your tongue curled inward. Don't rush through this step, do it slowly.

- Next, exhale slowly through your nose.

- Repeat as many times as you wish, or do this exercise for five minutes daily.

As your body temperature lowers, your mind also calms down and eases your anxiety. This exercise is so beneficial for you that once you experience it, you will make it a part of your daily routine.

Bhramari-Humming Bee Exercise

They often use this breathing exercise to instantly calm anger and frustration. It involves using a humming sound whilst practicing the exercise. The bhramari breathing exercise is yoga, and it helps to soothe the area around your forehead, which relieves tension and stress. Here's how you conduct this exercise.

- Close your eyes and relax your facial muscles.

- Sit in a comfortable position, sitting upright. Don't slouch.

- Place your fingers on the tragus cartilage that covers your ear canal.

- Inhale deeply through your nose, keeping your mouth closed.

- As you exhale, gently press down on your tragus.

- Make a loud humming sound while doing this exercise.

- Repeat as many times as necessary.

Due to the loud humming sounds that may disturb those around you, find a quiet, private space to perform this exercise. You can practice this exercise along with your friends and family, provided that you focus on the technique.

Numbered Breathing Exercise

Numbered breathing exercise is commonly used to help people gain control over their breathing. It helps to reset your mind and eliminate any negative thoughts and energy; however, this exercise might cause anxiety in people who have anxiety disorders, so start small and see how it goes. Here are the steps below.

- Close your eyes and sit or stand upright, whichever you prefer.

- Inhale through your nose until you have reached your limit and can't take in any more air. Don't do this quickly, do it slowly so that your lungs don't fill up too fast.

- Exhale slowly until all the air has left your lungs.

- Inhale again, using the same approach. Make sure that your eyes are still closed.

- Hold the air inside your lungs for a few seconds before you exhale.

- That would be counted as breath one.

- Inhale to your limit again.

- Keep it in for a few seconds and then let it out.

- That would be counted as breath two.

- Repeat these steps until you have completed 10 breaths.

You can count higher if you feel comfortable, or you can count lower if you are feeling overwhelmed. Start with a small number until your body becomes accustomed to performing this exercise.

Anxiety and Breathing Exercises

People who suffer from anxiety may become anxious when performing these exercises, especially if they don't have any previous experience with breathing exercises. Focusing on your breathing may cause a certain amount of anxiety to build up, hence you must practice daily to overcome this. When people are anxious or when they face a situation that stresses them out or causes fear, breathing exercises can help them calm down, if used correctly. During a panic attack, people take rapid, shallow breaths that come from their chest. This is also known as thoracic breathing, and it upsets the levels of oxygen and carbon dioxide in your body.

When this happens, your heart rate increases, you become dizzy and light-headed, and you experience tension in your muscles. These signs show that your blood isn't receiving a good amount of oxygen, and this triggers a stress response from your body. Your panic attack would instantly blow up because of the increased anxiety caused by the stress response. Diaphragmatic breathing, also popularly known as deep breathing, stimulates the nervous system that regulates blood flow, heartbeat, digestion, and breathing. Deep breathing helps to avoid the fight-or-flight response that comes with stress and anxiety. We have highlighted the top 10 breathing exercises above, so choose the ones that you feel comfortable doing regularly. You should never have to force yourself to do any of these exercises. If you are doing it, do it willingly and enthusiastically. Next, we are going to talk about meditation and how it works wonders in eliminating negativity from your life.

Meditation and Yoga

Millions of people use mediation and yoga worldwide to help deal with stress and maintain a healthy mind and body. The benefits of yoga and meditation cannot go unappreciated, as the results have spoken for themselves in the lives of so many people. Celebrities have sung the praises of yoga and meditation for years now, claiming that yoga maintained their healthy bodies and splendid figure. Meditation and yoga can help you achieve a positive mindset by eradicating negative thoughts and emotions.

How Do Meditation and Yoga Benefit Your Mind and Body?

Yoga is a holistic practice that involves body movements,

breathing, meditation, and mindfulness to help you achieve a healthier lifestyle. In this chaotic world we are living in, it's hard to keep up with all the stress and drama that unfolds daily in our lives. Our mind, like a sponge, absorbs the negative emotions, the bad vibes, and the traumatic experiences that we encounter. Over time, our minds become weak and cannot carry the mental load any longer, which causes emotional exhaustion and an array of other mental health issues. This is where yoga and meditation help lift this load and free you from the burden of negativity. Here's how yoga and meditation can benefit your life.

Yoga Promotes Physical Movement and Strength

It's important to be physically active and healthy in life. Most people lead lives that involve work, home, and back to work again. There isn't any time to exercise or to even take a walk to stretch out those legs. As a result, the muscles become stiff and flexibility no longer exists. Yoga can help to warm up those muscles and get the blood pumping to all the right places. By doing it regularly, your body becomes flexible and your core muscle strength gets renewed.

Yoga Helps to Ease Back and Joint Pain

Pain is something we all feel regardless of our age. Eventually, our joints and our bones wear out as we age, and painkillers can only work for a certain amount of time. If you are experiencing any pain in your joints or in your body such as lower back pain or cramps, consider using yoga to help treat your pain. Yoga can soothe aching joints and take care of the root of the problem in the long term. If you practice yoga daily, aching joints and nagging back pain will become a thing of the past. All the poses and stretches help keep your joints well oiled and working properly. Even your back pain would disappear as your posture corrects itself through the daily use of yoga.

Yoga Improves Your Sleep

Yoga relaxes you and helps to keep your mind calm, which is necessary for you to fall asleep and stay asleep throughout the night. People have developed issues with their sleep because of stress, depression, anxiety, staying up late with a newborn, studying for a test, or working jobs that require them to be awake at odd hours. Whatever the reason may be, once your sleep routine has been altered, it can have lasting effects for months on end. You can use yoga to help you get back your love of sleep. Since it is all-natural, there are greater chances of your sleep issues being sorted out permanently.

Yoga Helps to Regulate Your Moods

If you are the type of person who is always moody and controlled by your emotions, then yoga could be the answer that you were looking for. People who practice yoga on a daily basis feel much more in tune with themselves. Their physical energy levels increase, and they automatically gain a boost in their self-confidence and enthusiasm, making it difficult to fall into a negative mood. With a clearer mind and a positive outlook, you will regulate your moods healthily.

Meditation Can Aid in Healing

In certain instances, meditation has been used to help people heal from sickness and disease. The theory about mind over matter is 100% true. Once you gain control over your mind, you will also be able to control what goes on with your body. If your medical condition is related to or worsened by stress, then meditation is the right choice in finding a treatment for that condition. When you meditate, you are ridding your body of negative thoughts, overwhelming toxins, and unnecessary noise. With all the bad gone, there will be more space for healing and positivity.

Meditation Improves Your Decision-Making Abilities

We all struggle with deciding from time to time; however, when our mental state holds us back from making the right decision at the right time, we have to take action and correct it. You can use meditation to help you improve your decision-making abilities. If you have a logical mind, you will judge situations more easily. A logical mind is achieved through regular meditation to help get rid of the old and make a place for the new. You cannot think clearly if your mind is focusing on ten different things, and your ability to decide properly gets second-guessed.

Meditation Helps You Stay in Tune With Yourself

It's easy to lose yourself amid all the pressures of life. You eventually lose touch with who you really are, and when you look at yourself in the mirror, you don't recognize the person you see. Practicing mindful meditation will help you reconnect with your inner being. When you meditate, you put aside everything else that demands your attention. With no other disturbances, face yourself and deal with your issues head-on. Meditation allows you to make time for yourself, and you can start exploring your forgotten interests again, bringing back the things you loved doing before.

Meditation Strengthens Your Emotional Well-being

An overload of emotions can manifest negatively in different ways, especially when you don't have the time to deal with them healthily; however, when you meditate, your mind sorts through all the feelings and emotions that have built up inside. You make the time to give each of your emotions the attention they need, which helps you to work through them much easier. As you meditate regularly, you become emotionally stronger and more resilient. Your self-awareness increases, you become focused on the present, negative emotions will be reduced, you will gain new skills to manage your stress better, and you become more patient. Now you can face any situation with confidence that you will not become overwhelmed with emotions.

Different Meditation and Yoga Practices

Now that you are aware of the benefits that yoga and meditation have on your mind and body, you can make them a part of your life. There are so many types of meditation and yoga practices that are available today. We have listed the most popular practices that people all around the world use daily. Some might appeal to you, whilst others might not. You can choose the easier ones to start with so that you don't attempt anything that may be a bit too difficult for you. People make the mistake of choosing the most laborious exercises first, and when they cannot complete them, they give up and stop trying. Yoga and meditation are very similar, so if you are trying it for the first time, approach the practice with baby steps. Dip your feet in the shallow end and get a feel before you dive straight into it. Below, you will find the different yoga practices that are most widely used today.

Vinyasa Yoga

Even yoga is a type of meditation that involves a lot of body movements. It simply means "to place specially." It refers to placing our body in different ways during the yoga practice. All the poses done during a vinyasa session are coordinated with the help of your breathing. There is no break given in between poses. You flow from one pose to the next in a sequence without interruption. You can move at a rapid pace, or you could move slowly. It all depends on your preference. This is a great way to stay in tune with your yoga practice. During your session, your yoga instructor would say the word 'vinyasa,' which shows that you should start with a sun salutation.

You must start with a chaturanga, which is like a plank, and end with a downward-facing dog. If you find it difficult at first, try to follow along as well as you can. You don't have to force yourself to match the movements of others. You will get there eventually as you practice. This type of yoga is great for building strength and flexibility.

Hatha Yoga

Hatha yoga, a Sanskrit term, is a type of yoga that also involves a lot of physical movements. It is one of the most popular types of yoga used around the world today. With this type of yoga, you will be required to pair your movements with your breathing during a slow-paced yoga session. There are many health benefits of using hatha yoga, and one of the most common benefits are decreased anxiety levels, improved balance, and a clearer mind. It also helps to ease pain, reduce symptoms of menopause, and lower blood pressure. If you are a highly stressed-out person, hatha yoga would be a great place to start. We cannot compare a hatha yoga session to any other session because it differs from instructor to instructor and from person to person.

When you are starting a session, you will be required to start with a centering exercise. You can do this by sitting down or laying on your back, and the exercise will start with a few minutes of silence, a guided meditation, or a short breathing exercise. From there, they will instruct you to perform several distinct movements which involve a lot of bending, twisting, and folding. This yoga position also involves using breathing techniques along with physical movements in a timely manner.

Ashtanga Yoga

This type of yoga, also known as the eight limb path yoga, involves intense physical postures that target the eight limb paths of your body. They derived vinyasa yoga from ashtanga yoga, and both types of yoga work with the breath-movement process. It tests your mental and physical strength by using different yoga positions that are challenging. Ashtanga yoga is popular for being one of the most strenuous types of yoga, as it is decades old and was also used by the yogis. There are six different levels to complete in ashtanga yoga. The primary level, the secondary level, and four levels of the advanced stage. As a newbie to yoga, you would start with the primary level and gradually work your way up to the advanced levels.

This type of yoga is fast-paced and very energetic. Your body and mind are cleansed through the intense heat that is experienced during these ashtanga yoga sessions. The body is rid of impurities in the blood, and any joint pain is eased. The benefits of this type of yoga are seen instantly, and many people chose this as their main yoga exercise. Next, we will look at the different meditation practices that are used by people to achieve a positive mindset.

Mindfulness Meditation

Mindfulness meditation is a popular type of meditation that involves being aware of the present moment. When you are practicing this type of meditation, you pay attention to your thoughts as they show up in your mind. You don't judge them or react negatively toward them. Instead, you allow them to pass through your mind with no hesitation. As these different thoughts pass by, you scrutinize them, noting any patterns you notice. Concentrating on your thoughts whilst being aware of the present is how you practice this type of meditation. You can focus on an object such as a candle flame to help you concentrate, but most people prefer focusing on a moving object like fish swimming gracefully in a fish tank or the slow movements of plants dancing in the wind.

You don't need a teacher to guide you through the process of mindful meditation. You can do this on your own. As long as you have a quiet place to meditate, you can practice this type of meditation as frequently as you wish. Remember that you have the power to control your thoughts, regardless of what the situation is. Don't allow yourself to judge your thoughts. This is how the meditations become unfruitful.

Spiritual Meditation

Spiritual meditation involves meditating according to your own personal religious beliefs and faith. A Christian person would meditate on the bible or pray and worship. A Hindu person would choose to meditate using prayer beads or singing and chanting hymns. It doesn't matter what religion you belong to or what your beliefs are, meditating according to your faith is done at your own discretion and in your own special way. People who don't believe in spirituality won't take part in this type of meditation. Your belief and faith in God are what help you achieve a positive mindset through meditation. Spiritual meditation can be practiced in your place of worship, along with other members of your faith, or it could be conducted in your own home. You don't have to be guided by a pastor or priest; however, if that's what you prefer, then it can be arranged.

Movement Meditation

This is a universal type of meditation that doesn't involve any specific chanting or positioning to be a success. Anyone can do this meditation as it can be a part of your daily life. It involves doing things you would normally do to relax or unwind after a long and stressful day. You can do movement meditation by taking a relaxing walk, doing a bit of gardening, or participating in gentle contemporary dance. Qigong is another form of movement meditation that the Chinese people have practiced for centuries. This type of meditation has aided in healing sickness and promoting health. It involves well-structured gentle movements with meditation and breathing.

Movement meditation helps you connect with your body on a deeper level and keeps you focused on the present moment. Sometimes, we unknowingly fall into a state of meditation whenever we are talking on a quiet walk or watering the plants. These activities make us feel so relaxed, and we don't even realize it.

Loving-Kindness Meditation

This type of meditation is used to help people strengthen their emotions and feelings toward others and toward themselves. Emotions like compassion, kindness, and acceptance are all crucial to the well-being of a person's mental health and happiness. Sometimes people are closed off toward accepting and giving love to others because of emotional trauma that they might have experienced in the past. Meditation can help them open themselves up to connecting with others emotionally. If you cannot show yourself love, how will you accept love from anyone else? By doing this type of meditation, you are also healing and learning to love yourself more. You should make this meditation a part of your daily lifestyle. Speaking words of affirmation over yourself is one of the key actions that is required.

How to Get Started With Yoga and Meditation

You need little to start your journey with meditation and yoga. If you are serious about making it a part of your daily routine, then all you require is time. If you are not a very busy person, sit for an hour, quietly focusing on your breath. There should be no disturbances around or any noises that could distract you from focusing on your goal. If you lead a busy lifestyle, then you don't have to spend an hour involved in meditation. You can spend just 20 to 30 minutes a day focused on meditating. Choose your appropriate style of meditating. Whether it's the spiritual meditation or the mindfulness meditation, you must be prepared to do it wholeheartedly. The same rule applies with yoga, although it is more beneficial when conducted in the early mornings.

Prepare your mind beforehand for the meditation and yoga session. If a certain event deeply troubled you, try to calm yourself down before attempting to meditate. Going into a session without having the correct mindset will not bear any fruit. The goals you wish to achieve through meditating must be clearly defined prior to the session. If you know what you want, you will work harder to achieve it. Without a purpose, you would not be committed or focused on the meditation process. Make sure that you outline your objectives and your goals before you get started. Warming up your body before a yoga session is very important to prevent injuries. It would be good to work with an instructor if you are doing yoga for the first time.

In Closing

Yoga and meditation aren't something embraced by too many

people. The idea of sitting down quietly and doing nothing for an hour might seem like total nonsense to some people; however, the importance of spending that quality time on your own cannot be stressed enough. Meditation and yoga enable you to shift your focus on everything else and direct it to do what's essential now. Make the time to focus on yourself. This is a healthy way of helping you flush out the negativity and inducing positivity. If you are not familiar with yoga or meditation, do not fear giving it a shot. You will never know unless you try it, so be open-minded and try your best to make your journey a success.

CHAPTER 6

Step Five—
Learning to Love Yourself

We just need to be kinder to ourselves. If we treated ourselves the way we treated our best friend, can you imagine how much better off we would be?
—Meghan Markle

Positive Affirmations and Advice on How to Love Yourself

Congratulations! You're one step closer to achieving your goal. We have saved the best for last—learning how to love yourself. This step is as necessary as the others, so give it your all. Loving yourself is a topic that isn't discussed much, mainly because there are so many people who just don't care about themselves. When we talk about self-care, we don't just focus on your outer appearance. We assume that self-care means we should join the gym to become physically fit and dress well to look good; however, there are other things that go into taking care of ourselves. Your inner well-being is just as important as your outer well-being. Your emotions and your mental health should be a priority as well. In this chapter, we will explore the different aspects of self-care.

Self-Love for Dummies

Loving yourself is a tough task. It can even become annoying because of all the work that goes into it. There could be several reasons you wouldn't have the time to take care of yourself. Maybe you spend all day working and taking care of others, and by the time you are done, you have no energy left to focus on yourself. Let's look at Christine's life as an example. Christine was a working mom who had three kids. She worked Monday to Friday, and she only got off work in the evenings. When she comes home, she prepares for supper. She puts the kids' uniforms in the laundry, cleans up the house, and helps with homework. By the time her husband gets back from his job, the house is cleaned, the kids are fed and put to bed, and the table is laid out for him to have his meal.

Christine doesn't believe in asking for help. She thinks she can do it all as a woman; however, she gets frustrated a lot these days because she has been neglecting herself. By the time she goes to bed, Christine is already exhausted from a full day of working and taking care of everyone else. Her daily routine does not include any time for herself, and this is affecting her physically and emotionally. As the days go by, she becomes more and more tired. It shows in her outer appearance, and her demeanor changes around the kids. She becomes more irritable, and she loses her temper more often. This impacts the way she raises her children and how she interacts with her husband. Soon, things get out of control, and Christine is left emotionally and physically exhausted. This could be avoided if only Christine allowed her husband to help her around the house.

There are so many people out there who share similar experiences with Christine. Both men and women go through the daily pressure of life, kids, work, friends, and bills. These are all common issues that take up so much of our time. We spend so much of our time tending to the needs of others that we neglect our own health and well-being. There is a constant need for approval and acceptance that we all share as human beings. This makes us so involved in doing what everyone else wants, rather than focusing on what we want, and this is where the problem lies.

Why Is It So Important to Love Yourself?

Self-love is the key ingredient to living a fulfilling life. Have you ever stopped to think about how your inner self influences your outer world? I guess not, and to be honest, I don't think there are many people out there today who have stopped to think about this. For most people, thinking about these kinds of things seems too complicated and nerve-wracking, so they choose to overlook it completely; however, this topic should be explored, as it is crucial to you living a well-balanced life. It's time you put yourself first. Stop feeling guilty about the decisions you make for yourself. If you don't put yourself first, you can never give anyone else your 100%. Below, we highlight the importance of self-love, take some time to go through it and understand its importance.

Self-Love Fills in the Gaps

You will come across different relationships in your lifetime—family, friends, and lovers—relationships exist in all three areas. Not all relationships will work out. People will come into your life and leave a mark when they go. This causes a lot of hurt and pain, which can easily affect your self-confidence. If you don't have self-love, the hurt that you experience from these broken relationships can cause a lot of emotional damage. But if you are someone who loves yourself and if you nurture your emotions, you will fill the gaps that people leave when they walk out of your life. You will understand your worth, and the actions of others won't easily sway you. Loving yourself will get you through every heartbreak, no matter how bad.

Self-Love Helps You to Make Good Decisions

Every critically terrible decision that we make in life seems to come from a place of hurt and anger. No one has ever chosen to make the wrong decisions in a positive mindset. When you love someone, you will do whatever it takes to make sure that they are happy and taken care of. You would never make a decision that would hurt them or cause them to become unhappy. Similarly, when you love yourself, you hold yourself in high esteem. You wouldn't do anything that would upset your life or cause you harm. Every decision you make will benefit your happiness. Healthier decisions equal a healthier lifestyle and a happier you.

Self-Love Motivates You to Push Forward in Life

Life can knock you off your feet with no warning. One moment you are living the life you always wanted, and the next minute you find yourself knocked to the ground, unable to wake yourself up. Most people remain in that situation, unable to come out of it because they lack confidence in themselves. They don't believe that they are good enough to push through, and they don't feel like they are worth all the hard work that goes into starting life afresh. There are thousands of people living on the streets. Some of them are trying their best to climb out of that poverty, whilst others are content with living that way. They have accepted that life because they don't believe in themselves anymore; however, when you have love and respect for yourself, you will not settle for failure. You will push through and motivate yourself because you believe you deserve the best.

How to Love Yourself

Don't worry, it doesn't take a rocket scientist to understand how self-love works. You can start practicing self-love today. You don't have to possess a special talent or have a certain amount of money in your bank account. All you really need is a positive attitude and a little time set aside for yourself every day. Here are some great tips to help you love yourself every day. Start small, and do only what you can. Don't take on too much. You should be willing and open to change, only then will you learn how to love yourself.

Nourish Your Mind and Body

One of the most basic, yet most important aspects of self-care is making sure that your mind and body are being properly nourished. Skipping out on meals because you are so busy during the day or not getting the proper nutrients and vitamins from your food causes you to become physically and mentally drained. People neglect themselves because of working full-time jobs or being so consumed by the opinions of others that they purposely avoid eating certain foods just to please others. If you are practicing healthy eating because you are trying to achieve a healthy body, then there are certain diets you can follow so that you don't miss out on any nutrients. But desiring a skinny figure and starving yourself on purpose to achieve this will only cause more harm than good. When you value yourself, you would do nothing that would harm your body just to please others.

It is important to eat on time. It doesn't matter if you are at work or home, You should make yourself a priority and take your breaks when needed. Listen to your body and do what it is asking you to do. Drink lots of water, cut down on the junk and eat healthy foods that are rich in essential vitamins and minerals. You should also try to limit your alcohol intake and make time to exercise regularly.

Spoil Yourself

Make time to spoil yourself when necessary. Take yourself out on a date by booking a relaxing day at the spa or treating yourself to a new outfit. You don't have to spend a lot of money or you can try saving up money for your special treat day to go all out. Apart from those things, there are other ways to spoil yourself, provided that you enjoy these inexpensive spoils. You can bake yourself a batch of chocolate brownies or run yourself a nice hot bubble bath. You can also treat yourself to a day with no household chores. Your special treat days will be planned according to your preferences and budget. You don't have to go overboard if you cannot afford it. With proper planning and execution, you will be successful in making sure that you get what you desire. When people don't reward themselves from time to time, they become unmotivated in life.

Eventually, they lose the desire to work hard and push forward because they cannot reap the benefits. Can you imagine working hard the entire week? You put in the extra effort, you go to work on time, and you perform your best every day, but when you get your salary, all you do is pay bills? Who would be motivated to go to work every day? No one! But if you set aside some time and money for yourself, it would motivate you to go to work and still do your best.

Keep a Gratitude Journal

Once again, the benefits of journaling cannot go unnoticed. Having a gratitude journal at your disposal is the best way to help you keep track of everything that is good in your life when you need a reminder. Being reminded of all the blessings you have makes you more thankful and humble toward life. Try to write at least three things you are grateful for every day. This will train your brain to think more positively, and when you adapt to a positive mindset, you become more content and happy with your life. You don't have to constantly write in your journal, you can choose three days a week to do so. If you have to force yourself to do this, it will defeat the purpose of keeping a gratitude journal, so try to write only when you are inspired to do so.

Express Yourself

I cannot stress enough the importance of expressing yourself. Expressing yourself is crucial to your emotional well-being. If you are the type of person who bottles up their emotions and hides behind a fake smile, then you are heading for trouble soon. When you close up yourself and keep it all inside, you are allowing these feelings to eat away at your peace and happiness. Eventually, there will be nothing left of you to offer anyone else, and all your relationships will suffer because of this. Emotions are meant to be expressed, or else why would we have them? Your anger, frustrations, jealousy, love, passion, and happiness are all important emotions that make up your very personality. Some people don't know how to express themselves, so they lash out at others or get involved in drugs and alcohol to help them get rid of all the pain they keep bottled inside.

There are healthy ways that you can express yourself. As previously discussed, you can use a diary or journal to write about your feelings, or you could take part in various activities such as dancing or bodybuilding. When someone you care about is making you feel unhappy, instead of keeping everything inside and yelling suddenly, you should express your feelings by talking calmly or writing about them a letter and handing it to the person you are having issues with. Try using a different approach to expressing your emotions. It will help you gain more control over your feelings.

Improve Your Spirituality

Not everyone believes in a higher power, but for those people who do, focusing on their spirituality can really have a great impact on their self-love abilities. Getting in touch with your spiritual side helps you understand your purpose in life more deeply. When you establish a relationship with God, you see yourself through his eyes. You will come to understand that you were created with love and that you were sent to this earth for a purpose. Where there is spirituality, there will be positivity. And when you have a positive attitude, you will always see the best in others and in yourself. Your spirituality will enable you to open yourself up to experience life without the fear of failing or getting hurt. When you have a spiritual mindset, you always have peace during your trials. And when you have peace, you can face any situation with a smile because you know that there is a higher power who is taking care of your every need. This type of positive attitude will keep your mind healthy and optimistic.

These are just a few ways that you can show yourself love. I'm sure that you probably have your own special ways to spoil yourself; however, you might not have the time to do so. It's time you stop placing everyone else's needs above your own. If you are not happy and healthy, how will you make sure that everyone else is? As the famous saying goes, "You cannot pour out of an empty cup," so you cannot give to others what you don't have for yourself. Use the advice given above, and show yourself love and respect. I know it can be difficult to put yourself first after years of pleasing everyone else. You wouldn't know where to start or what steps to take. Fear not. Below you will find the guidance you need to love yourself again. The steps mentioned below help you get started on your journey, so prepare your heart and your mind to receive this advice.

The Six-Step Process to Self-Love

Nothing is impossible to achieve as long as you follow a process. When you set a process for yourself to follow, everything becomes more clearly defined because you can follow a well-directed path that leads you to your goals. Planning is essential to getting things done the right way. You plan for risks in case something happens, and you need to have a backup plan in motion. You also plan so that you become more confident in your actions because you understand what you are doing. Below, we have listed six steps to help you learn how to love yourself. If you surrender to these six steps, you will love and respect yourself every day.

Step One: Accept Responsibility for Your Feelings and Be Willing to Experience Pain

The first step in learning to love yourself is to accept responsibility for your feelings. You understand that things are not always going to go your way. There will be instances where you have to surrender and go with the flow. Accepting your feelings and emotions for what they truly are can be a scary process, but it has to be done. When you take responsibility, you are opening yourself up to correction for your own good which will enable you to become stronger and wiser. Another important aspect of loving yourself is preparing yourself for future hurts and pain. When you think about the future, you shouldn't only imagine those fairy tales. You must also keep in mind that there will be people who are going to hurt you in the future. When you learn to accept the pain, it won't come as a shock so much to you the next time around, so you won't be too hard on yourself.

When we don't prepare ourselves for pain, it can damage our

131

self-confidence, which is necessary for self-love. The more we ignore certain aspects of our lives, the more power they gain over us. Confronting your emotions and accepting responsibility for your actions is the best way to take back your power.

Step Two: Develop a Learning Attitude

Life is one big lesson that we all have to endure. There are many tests and trials that show up along the way, and the manner in which we handle these tests determines what the outcome will be. In all that you encounter—every problem, every failure, every heartbreak—open up yourself to learn as much as you can from those experiences. When you develop a learning attitude, you become wiser and more responsible in the decisions that you make. Instead of wasting away your time being sad over these things, you can choose to understand what went wrong and why so that you can avoid this in the future. People nowadays don't understand how important it is to take away lessons from everything that happens in life. They would rather choose to become vengeful or bitter about their tough experiences.

How is that going to help you in life? How is the anger and bitterness going to make life better for you? Use a different approach from now onward. Don't let your emotions cloud your ability to grow and learn from your mistakes. Humble yourself and put your pride aside. A wiser version of yourself is better than a foolish version of yourself. This is also self-love.

Step Three: Stay Away From Situations and People Who Bring You Down

Not everyone who comes into your life has your best interests at heart. There will be people who are ever ready to bring you down and take pleasure in seeing you fail. It could be your friends, your family, and even people you don't know, better known as "silent haters." These people mask their jealousy and hatred with fake smiles and shows of affection. After gaining your trust, they manipulate you and take advantage of your kindness. You need to identify who these people are by interacting with them. Here are some tips to help you identify toxic people in your life.

Signs to Look Out for When Dealing With Toxic People

- You are always confused about the person's behavior.

- Whenever you tell them about your achievements, they downplay it as something small.

- You feel you always have to defend yourself when you are with this person.

- Their true intentions are rarely revealed, and you always question their motives.

- They make you feel guilty about things you never did.

- When you are happy, they are not around to celebrate with you.

- You always feel emotionally drained whenever you are around them.

These are common signs to look out for in toxic people. The moment you notice these signs, remove yourself from that toxic environment. Cut off all ties with bad friends, distance yourself from family members who may be toxic, and stay away from situations that cause you undue stress and tension. Freeing yourself from negative influences is the best way to protect your peace.

Step Four: Make Time to Work on Your Dreams

Your dreams hold a great deal of importance to you. They keep you motivated, and they give you something special to look forward to in life. If you push them aside and pay no attention to them, eventually your dreams will lose their importance. Remember that your dreams are a part of who you are, so you should make time to work on them. Sometimes our goals and objectives may change according to our situations, so it is necessary that we make time to alter them and update them as we go along. Don't forget about your goals and dreams. Without them, life would have no meaning or purpose. When you achieve your goals, you become a happier person. You feel more content and fulfilled in life because you achieved your goals.

When you ignore your dreams, you are unknowingly ignoring a part of yourself. Letting your dreams die because you have been making other things a priority is like letting a part of yourself die as well. How is that practicing self-love? Killing your hopes and aspirations is far from loving yourself. It's time to get things in order and make yourself a priority. Love yourself enough to work on your dreams and make them a reality.

Step Five: Take Action

It's time to get the ball rolling and put your plans into action. Whatever you have done for yourself thus far, now is the time to do good on your word. Now that you have a better understanding of what self-love entails, start working on step one of this six-step process. Draw up a plan to help you stay focused on learning to love yourself. Try to fit in some 'me' time into your daily schedule, whether you're working or at home. The day can get hectic, and it becomes easy to forget about yourself whilst focusing on several things. Stop putting it off for the next day or the next week. The longer you wait to make a change, the greater the chance of you forgetting about it altogether. Get rid of the excuses and do something good for yourself right now!

Step Six: Evaluate and Track Your Progress

Once you have followed through with the plans you have made, ensure that you are tracking your progress in a journal. Ask yourself the following questions to help you determine if your plan is working, or whether you have to change it. Here are some questions you can ask yourself when evaluating your progress.

- Are you spending at least an hour focusing on yourself these days?

- Do you see a change in your emotions or in your overall demeanor?

- What has changed since you started making time for yourself?

- How has this change benefited you?

- What were some problems you have encountered so far?

- How have you dealt with these issues?

- Do you think that there is anything you should change?

- If so, what needs to be changed?

Your next plan of action will depend on your answers to the above questions. Answer them truthfully and honestly. If you have experienced any fallbacks or obstacles along the way, make a note of it so that next time you will know what to expect. You should review your progress weekly. This will help you find any patterns that may point to a potential concern.

In Closing

Loving yourself is the ultimate key to achieving a healthy and positive mindset. When you are happy and feeling good, you will see the world from a different angle. This angle is necessary for you to live your life to the fullest without holding back. Remember that it will not be easy, especially if you are a person with low self-esteem. It takes a lot of hard work and dedication to climb up out of the depression and bad routines. But when you are ready to make a change, nothing else will stand in your way. No one is ever going to understand what you are feeling, except for yourself because you are your own best friend. You know what you need and you understand what it would take to make you happy. You are your own best friend. When people let you down and disregard you, the only thing you can do is pick yourself up and continue pushing on. You deserve to love yourself and spoil yourself from time to time.

CHAPTER 7

Positive Affirmations for a Healthy Mindset and Attitude

Daily Affirmations and Words of Encouragement

Everyone needs a bit of encouragement and motivation on their journey, and you are no different in this case. You have embarked on a five-step journey to a healthier mindset, and this is no simple task. You will encounter several obstacles along the way, and you will need the motivation to help you stay focused on your journey. We have created a daily affirmation guide that will help you stay hopeful, no matter what may come your way. Embrace this short guide and use it to help you push through the hard places on your journey.

Positive Affirmations to Keep You Motivated in All Areas of Life

Are you ready to transform your life? If your answer is yes, then make use of these daily affirmations to help you along the way. We have grouped affirmations according to different categories of life, so focus on the category that you are working on at the moment.

Daily Affirmations About Relationships and Love

- I am surrounded by people who love me and I feel blessed.

- I attract true love and respect.

- All of my relationships are filled with love, and they will last long.

- I deserve to be loved, treasured, and cared for.

- I look at everything in my life through loving eyes. I love everything I see.

- There is no room for hatred in my heart. I love everyone I meet.

- I am blessed with an amazing wife, husband, and children.

- I am blessed with incredible parents and siblings.

- My friendships are important to me, and I cherish all of my friends.

- I have peace and harmony in my relationships.

- I am loyal, dedicated, and loving toward my friends and family.

- People can always depend on me. I am always available to help.

- My relationships are healthy and vibrant.

- There is no room for lies or dishonesty among family members.

- I radiate love and happiness wherever I go.

Daily Affirmations About Forgiveness and Gratitude

- I am grateful for everything that I have, and I will always be grateful.

- I will focus my thoughts on positivity and gratitude.

- I have let go of everything that had pained me in the past.

- Today is a new day, and the mistakes I made stay in the past.

- I am always grateful for the small things in life. I understand their importance.

- I am so thankful for my family and my friends.

- I understand all the ill feelings inside me that I have toward anyone else, and I let go of all these negative emotions.

- Whatever people have said about me, I forgive them for it.

- I forgive those who hurt me and left me when I needed them.

- The doors of my heart are open to renewing my relationships with others.

- We can solve every problem with love, no matter how big or small.

- With each new day comes a new opportunity to do good and live right.

- I choose to forgive and forget so that I may have peace.

Daily Affirmations About Self-Worth

- I am worthy of love and respect.

- I will express myself in a healthy and positive way.

- I am gentle, caring, and helpful toward others.

- I can make my dreams a reality.

- I choose happiness.

- I choose peace.

- I radiate positivity wherever I go.

- I forgive myself for all the things I have done wrong in the past.

- I am my biggest supporter in any situation.

- I do not entertain any negative thoughts about myself.

- The opinions of others don't dictate who I am.

- If I fail at any task, I will get back up to start again.

- My failure does not influence my abilities.

- I am more than a and I can achieve all my goals.

Daily Affirmations About Health

- Each day, I grow healthier.

- I am filled with energy, and I can do everything I put my mind to.

- I always think positively, and my actions are in line with my beliefs.

- Every cell in my body is healthy and working well.

- I can overcome any sickness or disease.

- I will not succumb to any physical illness or pain. I am stronger than I think.

- I treat my body as a temple. It is clean and free from negativity.

- I am free from all sickness. I have no diabetes, no heart conditions, no blood pressure problems, and I am free from cancer.

- There is no pain in my body. I am strong and fit to do anything I want.

- Every disease, body rash, allergies, and discomfort will cease to exist.

- I exercise daily and eat healthy foods to promote my well-being.

In Closing

Use these positive affirmations daily by speaking them out loud, and be passionate about the words you are speaking into your life. You become what you say you are, so always try to say positive things about yourself. You can overcome the negativity in your mind by confessing positive words with your mouth. Believe in these affirmations, and they will become a reality in your life.

Conclusion

Here you have it. The five steps to achieving a positive and healthy lifestyle! You can finally take charge of your mind after learning to use a positive approach rather than a negative approach toward situations that occur in your life. All the tools you need to change your attitude and mindset have been provided to you in this book. The only thing you have to do is put the plan into action and start the process. Remember, nothing is impossible to achieve when you are determined to see a change. The benefits of positivity are hard to miss, and we should strive daily to eliminate negativity from our lives so that we can reap the sweet benefits of leading a positive lifestyle. By now, you're probably tired of living your life the same way, following the same routine and the same cycle repeatedly.

There comes a time when you have to say enough is enough, and get up off that comfortable throne of negativity. Initially, things might be difficult to adjust to; however, you will eventually get the hang of it. Stay focused and stay dedicated to this journey and ignore all kinds of negativity that may come your way. You will encounter distractions and obstacles that will try to divert you from your goal. Your success will depend on how well you deal with these obstacles. Now is the time. Prepare your mind, embrace the change, and start your journey to positivity. Stop making excuses and start desiring change more than ever before. For when you truly desire something, you will do whatever it takes to achieve it.

You can use journaling to help you plan and track the progress of your step-step journey. Doing this will help make this journey so much easier for you. Make use of all the tools we have provided, and take advantage of the amazing advice given to you through this book. Only you have the power to change your situation, no one else can do it for you. You cannot depend on your spouse, your parents, or even your kids to help you change your life. We only get one life to live. We cannot come back from the dead and make changes then, we have to do it whilst we are alive. Live with no regrets. If you want to do something to make your life more rewarding, then nothing should stop you from working toward that goal. Grab life by the horns and give it your best shot. You can defeat negativity, have faith in the process, and believe in yourself.

References

7 famous diary entries from extraordinary people. (n.d.). Paper republic EU. https://www.paper-republic.eu/blogs/paper-republic/7-famous-diary-entries

Ackerman, C. (2019a, July 10). *83 Benefits of journaling for depression, anxiety, and stress.* Positive psychology. https://positivepsychology.com/benefits-of-journaling/

Ackerman, C. (2019b, July 10). *83 Benefits of journaling for depression, anxiety, and stress.* Positive psychology. https://positivepsychology.com/benefits-of-journaling/

Ankrom, S. (2021, March 20). *How to breathe properly for relieving your anxiety.* Verywell mind. https://www.verywellmind.com/abdominal-breathing-2584115

Benefits of journaling: The science and philosophy behind keeping a diary. (n.d.). Intelligent change. https://www.intelligentchange.com/blogs/read/benefits-of-journaling

Brody, J. E. (2017, March 27). *A positive outlook may be good for your health.* The New York Times. https://www.nytimes.com/2017/03/27/well/live/positive-thinking-may-improve-health-and-extend-life.html#:~:text=Studies%20have%20shown%20an%20indisputable

Control quotes (1368 quotes). (n.d.). Goodreads. https://www.goodreads.com/quotes/tag/control

Cronkleton, E. (2019, April 9). *10 Breathing techniques.* Healthline. https://www.healthline.com/health/breathing-exercise

Failure quotes (2484 quotes). (2009). Goodreads. https://www.goodreads.com/quotes/tag/failure

Healthy mind quotes (33 quotes). (n.d.). Goodreads. https://www.goodreads.com/quotes/tag/healthy-mind

How to create a positive mindset and attitude in life. (n.d.). Intelligent change. https://www.intelligentchange.com/blogs/read/how-to-create-positive-mindset-and-attitude

Jeon, H. (2020, February 12). *The next time you face rejection, ask what you can learn from the experience.* Good housekeeping. https://www.goodhousekeeping.com/life/relationships/a30719895/how-to-deal-with-rejection/

Let loose, start living, and stop taking yourself so seriously. (2011, January 26). *You have a calling.* https://youhaveacalling.com/spirituality/let-loose-start-living-and-stop-taking-yourself-so-serious

Ludlam, J. (2020, September 28). *30 self-love quotes that celebrate the greatness of you.* Country living. https://www.countryliving.com/life/g29661464/self-love-quotes/

Mindful Staff. (2019, April 13). *How to Meditate.* Mindful. https://www.mindful.org/how-to-meditate/

October 6, H. E. U., & 2021. (2021, October 6). *How to deal with disappointment: 12 Helpful steps.* The positivity blog. https://www.positivityblog.com/deal-with-disappointment/

Positive quotes & sayings to brighten your day. (2021, May 7). Keep inspiring me. https://www.keepinspiring.me/positive-quotes-and-sayings/

Sherwood, A. (2018, January 26). *What is positive thinking?* WebMD. https://www.webmd.com/mental-health/positive-thinking-overview

The science behind breathwork. (2021, January 12). Backline. https://backline.care/science-breathwork/

Printed in Great Britain
by Amazon

18576115R00092